P
it i
but
it is an up to you.

Gold from the Well©

Jocelyn "Josh" Apo

As told to Julie Smutko Daugherty

With Michael Palumbos

I dedicate this book to my family, especially my mother for all the things she has done for me when I could not do for myself.

I thank God for my journey from Haiti to America. Without God in my heart I would not have made it. I learned about God from my mother who believes it is better to work first in order to feed her family. Only God gives us what we need.

Coming to America God blessed me with a wonderful family – my wife and kids. I love them very much and appreciate each one of them.

Mother, I love you dearly and thank you for believing in me.

Jocelyn Apo

Foreword

I had just listened to another of Josh's stories about his life in Haiti. It was so difficult for me to fathom how this incredible human being was able to smile, laugh and love as much as he did given all of the hard facts that made up his life. I looked at him and said, "Josh, you need to write a book." Without skipping a beat he gave me one of his heart-warming smiles and said, "That's why I am here, you're going to help me." And it turned out Josh had long dreamed of his story being told in a book...so it was decided, I was going to help this man tell his story because the world needs more people like Josh in it.

Whenever I talk about Josh to others I always tell them that he is the wealthiest man I know. When I tell them that he is a custodian at the school where my wife used to teach they get this look on their face that says...that doesn't compute. I then describe the Josh I have learned to know and respect so much. You see, Josh isn't a one percenter or financially wealthy by most American's standards but he is filled with gratitude, happiness and love. His smiles are contagious and his hugs could melt an iceberg. He is wealthy in all of the areas that truly matter.

I first met Josh in 2005. My wife, Victoria, and I needed some help around the yard and she insisted that we use Josh...a custodian at her school who is always hustling for side jobs. The entrepreneur in me loved that. Josh would show up with his million dollar smile and his team and before we knew it the work was done. I liked hiring Josh and his team because they worked hard and it made me feel good to give the work to someone that not only needed it but really earned it. Little did I know that it would just be the beginning of the many things I learned to respect about him.

When you first meet Josh you can't help but to feel like you have known him forever. There's always a huge smile, a strong handshake (that graduates into one of his wonderful hugs) and a friendly hello. Actually, a friendly hello doesn't do it justice…from Josh, it's "Hello handsome," "Hello my brother" or "Hello…you are so beautiful…it's so good to see you". He'll look at your wife, nodding his head in affirmation and say, "He is a handsome guy; isn't he?" Conversely, he'll look at the husband and say, "You're a lucky guy to be married to her; she's a special lady." Few people can make you feel as good as Josh with just a greeting. Every time Josh and his team would complete a job for us, I'd ask him what I owed him. Josh's response never changes, "Just pay me whatever you feel it was worth." After knowing him for several years I had to ask about his unique "billing system." Does it always work out well for you, I asked? **His response was perfect.** He shared this with me, "Most of the time it works out, other times not so much but very often people pay us more than I would have asked for and that makes up the difference in the long run. Some of the people we do work for cannot pay a lot and we still like to help them." We continued to talk about it and for Josh it was his faith and trust in God that he believed the money would flow exactly the way that it needed to over time, as long as he continued to work hard. As Josh says, "God is good and I am very thankful for everything he does for me."

For the people that Josh has touched and those he continually reaches they say, "Josh is good and I am thankful for having him in my life and everything he does for me." This is not to say Josh is perfect by any means, it's just that he has made a decision to bring happiness to those he interacts with…every day. Josh doesn't hold onto anger, disappointment or any negative thoughts for that matter. Those types of thoughts would get in the way of who he wants to be. To some people he may seem to be a caricature upon first meeting him, surreal even, but there comes a moment in everyone's relationship with Josh that you realize that he is truly genuine. He cares about everyone that crosses his path…it's his goal to make you smile and he usually does.

What makes Josh truly amazing to me is that regardless of his life events and circumstances, he is capable of letting go, moving on, yet he only worries about the things that he can control. I myself have to work hard to let go and move on when something happens; so I am a bit envious of Josh's ability. I have so much respect for Josh because in spite of everything that he has gone through during his life, he has accomplished so much. Today he is living proof of the American dream.

I spent hours interviewing him in order to learn more about his life. Josh and I are within ten years of each other, yet we had such extremes in our childhood. At the same time that Josh was working for his mere survival, I was in middle school and delivering newspapers. I never experienced hunger, heck, I never missed a meal. It makes me wonder how our lives could be so different. The other thing that really spoke volumes to me about Josh's story is that there were two common themes I heard throughout his life that really struck me. Josh is abundantly grateful to God and man. He would thank God for being alive even when he didn't eat, and he would be thankful when he had a meal. He was thankful for the lessons that he learned from people that treated him poorly, and he was thankful to all of those that have helped him through the years. Josh also believed from a very young age that he was predestined for wonderful things. He knew there was a better life and bigger things in store for him if he just had faith in God. I believe that Josh's abundance of gratitude and faith make him wealthy in those areas and because he already felt wealthy, other forms of wealth were drawn towards him…magnetically.

I've been involved in other book projects in my life, pertaining to my work in finance. I feared I didn't have the creative flare to tell Josh's story in the way it deserved to be told, but I also could not see a way to hire a professional writer. Josh and I decided to put it out into the Universe. Taking a page from his book, as it were, we would see what God brought us. Very soon, Michael Wahl, a teacher at Barker Road Middle School, told Josh, "I think I know just the person for you." Enter Julie Daugherty, a parent in the school and published author. Julie had also been moved by Josh's exuberance and eagerness to be helpful. She had also been charmed into hiring him and his guys for work around the house. She knew what his presence was in the district, and agreed that his was a story worth her time to tell – whatever financial gain that might or might not result. For the past two years, she has shaped our initial conversations, adding many more of her own with Josh, into this heartwarming work of narrative nonfiction.

Life is a matter of perspective. For Josh, being in a position in which he is able to send money back to his family in Haiti, provide for his own family here in the States, and own his home today is a huge change from the single room, dirt floor hut he lived in as a child. I'd dare say, Josh is financially wealthy compared to when he first came to the United States as a Haitian refugee, 36 years ago. As I see it, Josh is wealthy; wealthy in gratitude, love, faith, friends, family and financially. He is the richest man I know and I strive to be more like Josh.

Enjoy his story, I know I did.

Michael Palumbos

Introduction

The Island now known as Hispania was home to a native people in numbers estimated to have been between 100,000 and three million when Christopher Columbus landed there in 1492. This population was violently extinguished by the end of the 16th Century, through direct killing and inhuman enslavement by the Conquistadors. These Spaniards, as well as French and English buccaneers on the Western part of the island also began to import slaves from Africa. Formally becoming the French colony of Saint Domingue through a 1697 treaty (while the balance of the eastern part of the Island evolved into the Dominican Republic), the region now known as Haiti yielded a rich bounty for many years. The French-based language spoken there today, Creole, is a relic of this period. But rampant deforestation led to erosion and an ensuing stark drop in planation yields. This short-sightedness was answered only by increasing the slave population. Their count, at 500,000 outnumbered land owners ten to one by the end of the eighteenth century, though a social structure based directly on skin color (ie, degree of intermingling) took hold, and even a class dubbed, *affranchise*, themselves mullato, owned slaves. This group was granted citizenship by the revolutionary French government in 1791, but the "elite white" Europeans refused to recognize this, prompting a banding together of *affranchise* and slaves in uprise. This unlikely cooperation would carry forward, recognizable in the peasant class feeling protective of these social superiors. In succession, former slaves Leclerc, then Dessaline and Christophe, ultimately led Haiti to independence from a France under Napoleon Bonaparte in 1804.

The entire 19th century in Haiti consisted of unrest, revolving leadership often ending in overthrow, and violent contention with Santo Domingo (Dominican Republic). The century was consistently plagued by vast poverty and political oppression of the majority of its citizens. Under the Monroe doctrine, the United States established a financial and military presence (predominantly marines) for the first half of the 20th century. This presence led to a new constitution, re-establishment of upper mullato control, and an amendment for leadership by popular election by the time it ended in 1947.

The first stable leadership (though also threatened by overthrow) in the 20th century was the election of François Duvalier, or "Papa Doc". His success in designating himself 'President for Life' (a practice with a rich history in Haiti) was underpinned by the establishment of a military arm, the *Tontons Macoutes* or "Bogeymen" who used Voodoo to terrorize the population into a paranoid police state by 1960, when Jocelyn Apo was born. The regime, defined by corruption, the fleeing of professionals from the country, and ubiquitous human rights violations, led to the further international isolation of Haiti. In 1971 before his death, Papa Doc passed his self-gifted title to his 19-year-old son, Jean-Claude, or "Baby Doc." Though he sought and gained respect and aid from outside the country, Baby Doc's regime was not substantively different from his father's. Any tourism that might have rebounded was undermined by The U.S. Department of Agriculture's mass eradication of pigs bred for livelihood after an outbreak of African Swine Fever in the late 1970s (further hardship predominantly to the peasant class), and reports of an AIDS epidemic in the 1980s. Demonstration of Baby Doc's oppressive leadership included a *Tontons Macoutes* on the order of 15,000 men, and a $2 million wedding in 1980 while most of his country lived at the brink of starvation. Baby Doc was removed to France in 1986.

The ensuing thirty years in Haiti have seen further corruption, violence, only moderately successful international intervention, abject poverty, and devastating natural disaster.

Source: Encyclopedia Britannica Online

I. Life

I was born November 7, 1960, so I been here a long time. When I was born, it was only my mother and me. Nobody else around. In Haiti we have midwives, but they don't go to school. But it was just my mother and me, and when I got older, this make me very emotional that she have me all by herself. My mother name is Amancia Yzarak. I can't tell you how many times I tell this woman I love her. I love her. I love her. I love her. She's amazing. All her kids was born at home, never go to the hospital. None of us ever been to the hospital. Everybody was born at home. And she always mention God. Even when she doesn't have anything to feed us, she always want us to pray God, to thank God just because we see that day. And then, when we do find something to eat, she always say, 'say thank you to God and we eat today and we don't know for tomorrow.' And when you pray for something you need, it's going to come. There's no other way around it. It's going to come. And I thank God for everything He have done for me. Because what He have done for me is amazing. And what He have done, my mother always say nobody else can kill her but God. It's only God who can kill her. And she still say that now, today. And she said that right to her enemy. She said that right into their face. She said you cannot touch me. You cannot do nothing to me. Only person who can do something to me is God. That's how she is. She incredible. And she knew the same thing for me, nobody can do nothing to me. The only one who can do it is God.

1

And that woman, she gave me nice tools. I have the same belief. Same belief. I owe all to God. I try to do right thing with somebody. Always.

     Jocelyn squeezed his small, rugged toes into thick mud. The formerly dirt floor of his family's straw hut was transformed when two solid days of rain eventually found its way through the hay roof. Standing in only a frayed shirt, he bent over the ground-level makeshift bed that he shared with his baby sister, attempting with futility to suppress a scream. His mother never begrudged him expressions of pain. He might be discouraged from feelings of anger, of sadness, of self-pity, but never physical pain. She grasped the fecal-covered worm Jocelyn, 'Amos' to his mother, had discovered dangling from his tiny exposed rear end and she began to pull.

     "I drank the water from the puddle, Maman! I know I should not but I was so thirsty," Jocelyn tearfully apologized.

     "And you see, God has granted your wish for water, Amos. God loves you. Now hold still while I pull, and pray for God to spare you the pain, my son."

     With that, Amancia removed the parasite from her fourth born of five children – the only one who stood to outlive her.

* * *

One brother, he my Maman's first. He died little. One day my mother was going somewhere and that brother begged to go with her. My mother told him, "No you cannot go. Stay here, I will be back." My brother started crying. By the time my mother came back, she found him lying on the floor. She found out that he ate something bad. Until this day she does not really know what killed him, but she always felt bad for not taking him with her when she left home. They called the doctor to come over. The doctor told her that the baby ate something and that is what took the baby's life. To this day, my mother is still talking about this. Then I had a brother who died when he was seven. I was very little at that time. I don't know how he died, but I believe he passed away in a bucket of water. He was standing in a bucket of water. There wasn't too much water in it and he fell in it. Then one brother, he grow up and die a young man. But he played with me. I remember a little bit he played with me before he die.

Gold from the Well
Jocelyn Apo

.

II. Play

The only thing I was doing for fun growing up is as a young guy, climbed the trees and then go hide behind your house or someplace and the other kid can find you. And then, play in the dirt. And sometimes, we go play in the creek. That's how we got some of this bad water in our system too. And basically, that's our only fun. Because growing up in my country for those age and for those time, was not easy. Never have a toy. Never have clothes like pants. I usually, have a little shirt, but not pants, not shoes, nothing like that. I was growing up without none of those thing. I would have a t-shirt and sometimes without t-shirt, just no pants, no shirt at all. But that's the way it was for young boy and young girl. And now, we'd been playing around with each other for years and nothing happened. Nobody do any weird. And never hit and any bad thing happen in this moment. There was not much trouble, because they all will watch, the whole community, whole town, like over there where you live, everybody know who you are, everybody watching.

When the rain had passed, and the land began to be dry again, Teti (Tetilesse) walked the children to the bank of the receding creek. There he knelt, and gestured for Jocelyn and Marinath to do the same. Yenocen accompanied them at his mother's request that he learn, though he kept up an air of independence from the older man. Teti lifted stones carefully from the mud, and again gestured for them to do likewise. The memory of their prior lessons returned to Jocelyn, and he rubbed a few stones at a time between his hands to free the drying mud, then began making a small pile. Pleased with himself, he looked up with his 6-year-old toothless grin to Papa Teti for approval, receiving only a nod. Once a modest pile had grown, he began laying his grid.

"How many?"

"Five we do on hands, so six today," Teti responded quietly.

All three lay a grid with six stones across, ending at 10 rows. Marinath, only four years old, placed a stone in her mouth.

"Only when we are thirsty!" Jocelyn reminded her, and brushed mud from her mouth.

"You have six, then six more. Count, Yenocen," Teti instructed.

Jocelyn raced his finger across the stones that lay in front of him, counting silently. "Twelve," he blurted, knowing it would irk Yenocen, who was nearly a grown man.

Yenocen punched Josh in the arm, pushing him off balance from his squatted position, but this did not prevent Jocelyn's laughing in delight. One stern glance from Pap Teti, though, and Jocelyn covered his mouth with his freshly muddied hand, and scrambled back up.

The lesson went on like this. Four sixes. Eight sixes. Then two sevens. Six sevens. Counting and counting again. Then Papa Teti fired, "Try to remember the answers now. And tell me as quickly as you can." Jocelyn and Yenocen searched their grids, their memories for the answers. Marinath looked on and began to shout random numbers along with them, at times shouting even letters of the alphabet. Jocelyn was, once again, unable to control his laughter.

"Alright, go and play," Papa Teti shot Jocelyn a tired glance.

"Sorry, Papa," Jocelyn pleaded genuinely, "She is just so funny!"

"Yes, she is funny," Teti allowed. He looked at his daughter, the first of his own blood, and cupped her chin in his hand. Marinath was at first terrified at the gesture, then recognized the show of affection as such and grinned as widely as her brother had.

"Go!" Teti again commanded the older two. Yenocen stood, gave his brother a nod, and ran off in the direction of town where he lived and worked. Jocelyn, feeling rejected, knew that his place was with friends of his own age, so he trudged toward the banana tree, wondering if he might find Jean-Baptiste there today. After his ten minute walk in solitude, he heard shrieks of delight coming from the direction of the banana tree. He hid behind a bush, and the stones he had carried from his lessons took flight toward his friends.

The spray of stones hitting the banana tree – pulled sideways by the weight of the bananas and the boys at play – startled Michele and Jean-Baptiste from their game atop the trunk. They scrambled down and chased after Jocelyn who was unable to run very fast for all his laughing. The two tackled him to the ground and tickled him until he begged for mercy. Once freed, Jocelyn climbed up the banana tree trunk to where he had seen his friends, using his tiny frame to make it bounce.

"Woo hoo!" Jocelyn shouted, still full of energy from his spirited entrance. He managed to get the trunk moving in a small rhythm. Michele was quick to follow behind him, while Jean-Baptiste stooped to pick up a small machete from the tall grass.

"Why did you bring your father's machete?" Jocelyn asked, both impressed and frightened to see the tool.

"Father doesn't know," Jean Baptiste murmured, then shouted, "I will chop the tree! We can build something!" as he ran to the base of the trunk. The fairer skinned boy, even smaller than Jocelyn, scrambled toward the tree where it curved. Jocelyn increased the pace of his rhythm and the banana tree bowed lower and lower to the ground. The movement was increased even more as Jean

8

Baptiste took weak swings at the trunk behind them. Michele, tightly straddling the tree immediately behind Jocelyn, began to shout.

"Whoa, Jocelyn, I'm going to fall…" and with that, he slid around the tree, grabbing Jocelyn by the shoulders in a vain attempt to hold on. Both boys dropped into the tall grass below, their inner thighs a bit the worse for wear in the descent. They lay laughing in the grass a few moments, but Jocelyn resolved on another ride before his friend entirely removed their favorite plaything. As he stood beneath the rounded trunk, Jean Baptiste brought down the machete with his strongest blow yet. His tool severed the remainder of the trunk and came to rest squarely in Jocelyn's scull as he reached his full height. All three boys began to scream frantically, but Jean Baptiste found the presence of mind to tug lightly at the machete to release it.

Michele stared wide eyed as Jocelyn stumbled around a few moments, then, frightened, took off running toward his own home. Jocelyn reached a hand up to touch his own small head at the source of a tremendous pain, and felt a wet patch. Instinctively he brought his hand into view to discover it covered in scarlet, just as drops of blood began dripping down his forehead into his eyes. He was overcome with a sense of confusion and began to cry.

"Walk home, Jocelyn! Walk home slowly!" Jean Baptiste advised shrilly. Jocelyn looked up to see his friend, machete still in hand, staring at him with the same fear-struck expression Michele had worn before he bolted. Jocelyn sensed that Jean Baptiste would soon leave him too.

"Come with… Come with me, Jean Baptiste. I won't tell. Come with me, PLEASE!" Jocelyn begged through his tears. He attempted to walk, but was overcome with so profound a dizziness that he knew he was likely to fall without his friend's help. Blood continued to obscure his vision and he squeezed his eyes into exaggerated blinks under the bright afternoon sun, focusing intently on moving his body toward home.

"Okay, okay, but please don't tell!" Jean Baptiste agreed. He ran to his friend's side, placing his free arm around Jocelyn. With the outer hand he dragged the machete through the grass in a guilty attempt to remove his friend's blood from the blade.

They moved in this way for nearly half an hour, making stops when Jocelyn was too disoriented to keep on, his friend too weak to offer much support. Finally they arrived at Jocelyn's hut, and Jean Baptiste called out weakly as they arrived, "Miss Amancia, please come!" Presently, Amancia appeared in the doorway and was panic stricken at the sight of her crying son. She immediately noticed the machete in young Jean Baptiste's hand and the horror his fair face still betrayed.

"Thank you Jean Baptiste, you go on home now," she tried to say neutrally. "Go now."

As Jean Baptiste dragged himself away from Jocelyn, wearing much of his friend's blood on his own small shirt, Amancia rushed her son in to the bed and lay him down. She muttered to herself, cognizant of his listening, about the foolishness of young boys. Now exhausted, Jocelyn entered and departed consciousness in seamless spurts as his mother went outdoors and gathered bark from two different trees in a small grove nearby. She pounded and moistened the bark, cutting them to size to cover the injury on Josh's small skull, then wrapped it all in bits of rags and twine she had learned to conserve.

Dusk arrived, and Jocelyn enjoyed a few lucid moments as his mother lay on the bed beside him. Her thin, strong arms were wrapped around him, and she rocked him gently, whispering prayers over the top of his head. Her eyes remained closed; the rhythm of her body was almost trance-like until she felt his eyes flutter open against her the sensitive skin of her neck.

"You scared your Maman!" she scolded angrily, but nearly silently as she captured her Amos's gaze. "Never do this again, you naughty boy!"

Jocelyn was powerless over the tears that filled his eyes, but he was intent on reassuring his mother. Taught not to return her eye

11

contact as a show of respect, he stared down the bed at his own belly, now bared of the shirt he had covered with blood. Jocelyn knew in his heart of hearts he had done nothing wrong, but he also knew better than to point this out to his sweet Maman. He only said softly, "Yes, Maman."

As though she read this thought, she said to him, "That Jean Baptiste should NEVER have brought his father's machete to play. His father will be very angry with Jean Baptiste. We needn't say anything, because his father will come to know what has happened. Jean Baptiste has been punished enough, but his father will not see that. Jean Baptiste will remain your friend, but as God is in heaven, don't you dare let anyone swing a machete around you again!"

Jocelyn managed a small giggle at what should have been obvious to him in the first place, six years old or sixty. His mother held him tightly to her, whispered a last prayer over him through her own giggle, then instructed him sternly to sleep for as long as he could.

III.   Hunger

The school in Haiti, that's very important. And that's why, in Haiti, we lost but we probably not totally lost in education because we have a lot of smart people there, too. At that time, you have to pay three dollars to send your kid to a school.   The difficulty was for a lot of family is if they find the three dollars to pay for the school to go there for six month, and they need to get a uniform. They need to get the shoes. They need to get the pencil. They need to take a thing that you can carry your stuff you're gonna need for the school. And it wasn't easy. And when somebody have three dollars in their hand, they have a hundred other things they can do with it. And it's not like you have somebody like this country here, somebody will tell you, 'You gotta go to school. You gotta go to school, it's good for you. It's good for you. You're gonna learn. You're gonna do this. You're gonna do that.' Nobody over there to encourage you for something like that. So that's why the culture at that time. I went for a very short time. My family, sister, a lot of them went for a very short time. But our parent cannot afford to continue us going back and forth in the school, because you can pay for that six months or for that one year. When the time come to pay again, you don't have it. And if you don't have the money, you can't go to the school.

Jocelyn and Marinath both pulled at the stiff necklines of their uniforms once they knew they were safe from teacher's view. Each secretly celebrated that they didn't know when they would be able to return again. Being April, it was getting very hot in the school building, and sitting still had never been in Jocelyn's nature, even if he had been grateful to God for the opportunity to learn. But for the last two weeks, Maman had not even had as much as mais mouline[1] to offer them for a midday meal, and had encouraged them to find a mango on their walk. They had been unsuccessful, and each found it harder and harder to concentrate on lessons.

Teti's job at the sugarcane factory had been taken from him with no regard for the mouths he had to feed. Amancia did her best to make ends meet by washing clothes for that rare class of neighbors who could afford extra garments and bedclothes, yet did not employ household staff. Her own energy was depleting quickly. Not only was every morsel offered first to the children, but she walked miles each day to pick up the laundry, scrubbed it hard in the creek (where she had not seen fish in some time), carried it home still heavy with water so that it could be hung, then meticulously folded it slightly damp and laid it beneath her own mattress for two nights so that she could

---

[1]   Simple bread made of cornmeal

preserve the illusion that she was ironing. This was the only way each family member still had two biscuits at dinner.

When Jocelyn and Marinath arrived home, their mother did not look up from her folding. "To the creek with those uniforms," she reminded them. Once the children had rendered them clean, she would take them to town for sale. That might mean a bit of meat could be had, IF her children had taken the tender care she had instructed. Marinath jumped up with anticipation. Marinath loved the water, and especially on a hot day.

"Amos, watch out for your sister, and come straight back!" Then, looking up from her work for a moment, with softness in her eyes, Amancia reminded her children, "*Croiser les bras* – cross your arms and thank God for letting you go to school this year."

The children obeyed happily, chiming in unison, "Thank you, God, for letting us go to school this year, amen!" Marinath added, "And thank you for the creek on a hot day!" Amancia smiled weakly and added, "If you see Papa Teti, please respectfully ask him to come home with good news of work. I have prayed for him too."

"We will, Maman," Jocelyn kissed her on the cheek, grabbed his old shirt and Marinath her wrap, and out the door they ran. For a moment Jocelyn considered a foot race to the creek, but he thought better of it, knowing how weakened his sister was especially. Instead, he made jokes and funny faces all the way to make her laugh. They

15

were lively and refreshed as they washed their uniforms in the shallow water. Marinath tired of scrubbing and asked her brother to finish her uniform while she took up her job of fish-spotting; on another day she might not be very serious about the responsibility, but hunger made her determined. She tried not to be disappointed when they came away empty handed.

As they walked past their nearest neighbor's hut, an old woman their mother had warned them against poked her head out. She scurried over to the children and muttered, "you are too hungry" pushing mais mouline into their hands before they could object. She gave a warm, though toothless grin and for a moment Jocelyn and Marinath felt gratitude and trust as she scurried back away, glancing over her shoulder toward the Apos' home, expectant of their mother's intervention.

Jocelyn motioned for Marinath to run behind a bush. She whispered, "maybe we should ask Maman?"

"No!" Jocelyn whispered too loudly, though with less conviction in his voice than he intended. "We just know she will say we must throw them away."

"Please can we eat them? May I at least eat mine?" Marinath begged.

"No!" Jocelyn insisted. "I will tell Maman, Marinath!" With that, he regrettably threw his own mais mouline into the thickest part of the bush, saying under his breath, "Thank you, God, for a Maman who looks out for us." He gave Marinath so intimidating a glare that the hungry little girl bent and laid hers on the ground as well, knowing some small animal would eat better than she that night.

When they returned to the hut, Amancia was preparing a pot over the fire. A few of the clothes in her charge had stubborn stains requiring boiling water, so she must do what she could to maintain the meager household income, however hot the day. Teti appeared in the doorway and ceremoniously bestowed on each of the children a sugarcane. No one dared ask how he came by them; rather, Marinath lit up, believing that her deference to her mother's rules brought her an answer to her prayers.

Jocelyn gratefully lay down on his bed and stretched luxuriously. Chewing on his cane, he took his young mind to a favorite place of imagining – Carnival! Only once before had he been to Carnival, but he knew Maman would take them again. Music, dancing, and the brightly colored ribbons ten adults trailed as they danced around a tall pole. He knew it was the most magical time in Haiti, and believed there were surely places in the world where there was sugarcane and magic always.

17

"When I grow up, I am going to live in a *pays étranger*[2]," he blurted out to his parents. "Yes. I am going to live in *pays étranger* and buy one wife and it will be very clean where trucks do not make a big smoke and there will be many beautiful colors, and…" he stopped himself. He knew better than to meet their gaze, but he felt their curious stares. Amancia and Teti exchanged a shocked look.

Jocelyn saw his mother shaking her head in amusement and return to her task. He lay back with his sugarcane with dreams of his *pays étranger*.

[2]   Foreign country

IV. Voodoo

My country, they're very well known for Voodoo, they got a lot of magic over there. It is very powerful magic. Very powerful magic. So that magic, they use all the time. In Haiti, it's a lot of Voodoo. I think at least 75-80% in Haiti is Catholic but they all 100% doing the Voodoo. And they have all kinds of religion over there, but it is very small amount of religion. But they're all doing Voodoo. When somebody's sick, if you come over there in Haiti, if you steal something, they don't call the police. They go to Voodoo people and Voodoo people will tell them who did it.

Early memories made quite an impression on Jocelyn. He was a boy who learned lessons from every experience, particularly missteps, and would grow into a man eager for others to benefit from his own hard-learned lessons. All too many of these lessons involved bodily functions, such was the harshness of his environs.

As a very small boy, Jocelyn had been taught to go into a field to move his bowels. Over and again, this small job proved troublesome. First, he did not clean well, and got a rash. He was shown to use a leaf to clean himself. Next, he cleaned himself with the wrong sort of leaf, and developed a terrible itch. So bad was his itching that he would drag himself across the ground, getting soil where it ought not be. Believing plants to be his great mistake, he tried using rocks to cleanse himself, only to scratch and cut his tender anatomy, leaving him no better off than he was with a terrible itch, but running to the creek for relief. It was not remotely uncommon for a neighbor, friend, to pass by whilst Jocelyn was occupied, and adults, especially, would offer friendly advice. This act was not sacred, and sometimes even a shared experience if it were dark and a neighbor or family member felt the same urge. The darkness in rural Haiti at that time, especially on a cloudy night, could be terrifying. Still, Jocelyn was never quite sure whom to trust, and depended on his own trial and error.

Trial and error, and of course the guidance of his dear Maman when she was available to offer it. She would sympathetically giggle through each of his experiments, offer home remedies as taught to her by her mother, and her mother before her, and eventually help him to commit to memory which leaves were his friends.

Since Jocelyn had learned this lesson well, it came as a great surprise to both when, as a big boy, he fell very ill with symptoms most likely associated with this process going awry. After days of Jocelyn writhing in pain, passing in and out of consciousness, Amancia pooled every resource she could in order to pay the Voodoo man. Enlisting Teti to carry a miserable Jocelyn all the way, Amancia set out with dogged determination to seek a cure for her only son.

Happily, when his weakened eyes met the bright sunlight, he rested peacefully on Papa's back.

As they passed through the gates of the Voodoo man's property, Josh's eyes immediately opened. Whether the spot of shade or the promise of relief, he gave himself over mentally to the one person his mother seemed to trust. After a brief ceremony, Jocelyn was made to dance. He was weak and in pain, but Jocelyn moved exactly as he was told. Next he was taken to a sort of outdoor shower where water was poured over him ceremoniously. He was then permitted to lay down as the Voodoo man prepared a tea, served to him promptly in comparison with the *lavement* which was yet to come. The Voodoo man prepared a gallon of water with many different ingredients – mostly plants – and continued to boil down the solution over hours. He muttered incantations over the pot and over Jocelyn in turn. At last, what remained was the *lavement* which was finessed by the Voodoo man into a tube-like apparatus fashioned from leaves, and even more deftly finessed into Jocelyn's source of discomfort.

And they waited.

Jocelyn rested peacefully for a few moments. Relief was largely mental, believing the Voodoo man was finished with his magical manipulation of his small, frail body, and also believing in God's work through this man. Then quite suddenly God's work, in its most basic form, was swiftly carried out with an urgency Jocelyn had never known. He found the energy to rush to the nearest field for the intestinal cleansing of a lifetime. Amancia grinned for the health and relief of her son.

For what seemed like months to the boy, Jocelyn stayed with the Voodoo man day and night. His mother would pay him visits and stay for as long as she could while he was returned to health. One evening, as she spooned a broth for Jocelyn, he dared to catch her eyes.

"Are all Mamans as good as you, Maman?" he asked quite innocently.

"No, son, not all Mamans are as good as me, and some are better. The Lord sends you the Maman you are meant to have and that is all there is."

"I don't believe there could be a better Maman!" her Amos protested.

"Maybe not, Amos. There are things I wish I could do for you, give you, that I cannot," she insisted. "But I CAN teach you to work, and I CAN teach you to pray, and this is all you need in your life.

"My son, if you don't remember anything else, I want you to remember these words: *Pray* as though it is all up to God, but *work* as though it is all up to you."

Knowing the weight his mother had just given to this advice, Jocelyn turned the words over in his head. He found a place for them where he could always find them, like his memories of the Carnival.

"This is what YOU do, Maman! You pray as though it is all up to God, but you work as though it is all up to you. When we eat, you say '*croiser les bras*.' When we cannot eat, you say '*croiser les bras*.' When we start work we do it. When we finish work we do it. When we wake up in the morning and when we go to sleep at night we pray."

Amancia felt a great pride swell up inside her. Pride for her insightful son. Pride that he saw in HER what she wished to instill in him. And pride in herself for teaching him well.

Gold from the Well
Jocelyn Apo

V. Trust

We never get in any trouble. Any trouble, I used to get by myself. Sometimes, when they sent me to go get water from the well, the 'puit,' and they give me something we call it 'coco.' It's almost like a coconut. It looks like a coconut. But they sometimes told me, don't put too much water in it because it will be too heavy, I won't be able to carry it. It's a very small thing. It's the size of a coconut. But I was so little, and the coco very slippery, too. Every time I break one of them, I got a spanking. They tell me not to put too much water, and I never know how much to put in there. And it always broken by being so slippery in my hand. I tried to explain that— and when it broke, I left the rest of it but I take a piece with me so they can see it is broken, nobody taking it. I want adults to believe me, trust me. But you know, it's just those type of parents, they was kind of rough in those times. Because I can understand their frustration, too, because they was raised a certain way that is completely different than people today. Life was so very hard then.

Amancia was beginning to discover that she wasn't the only one to believe Jocelyn was special. She did not wish to play favorites among her children, knowing too well how hard life would be for her daughter, especially. But signs from men in town, both positive and negative, all pointed to a charmed life for her son.

Teti had found work again, and Amancia had the luxury of going into town for milled flour. On one occasion, when Jocelyn and Marinath accompanied her, she spotted Mr. Hermilus in the dry goods store. Mr. Hermilus owned a large farm and Amancia had heard he was a fair man. She knew it would not be proper to approach Mr. Hermilus, but she gave him a deferent smile when their eyes met. Mr. Hermilus returned the smile, then surveyed her unkempt children. Bending down on one knee, he motioned Jocelyn over to him.

Jocelyn looked quickly to his mother's face for approval and she granted it with a subtle nod. Now that he was ten years old, Jocelyn stood taller than Mr. Hermilus was on his knee.

"What is your name, boy?" Mr. Hermilus demanded gruffly.

"Jocelyn Apo, sir," he returned, his eyes respectfully on his own grubby toes.

"Jocelyn Apo, you are a boy that grown people trust, aren't you?"

Jocelyn did not know a proper response, but he nodded his head and quietly responded, "Yes sir."

Mr. Hermilus roughly grabbed Jocelyn's hand, which hung awkwardly at his side. "You keep this for your friend, Mr. Hermilus," the man ordered. Jocelyn spied the glint of a new coin before the man closed his own fingers over Jocelyn's. "I am going to come get it from you in three weeks, okay?"

Jocelyn again nodded and produced a "Yes, sir," just loud enough to be heard and considered respectful. At that moment, his mother's cousin, Najac appeared in the doorway of the store. He made his way quietly to the counter where Amancia was paying for her flour, and trying very hard not to stare in the direction of the stranger and her son.

"Tomorrow is laundry, isn't it, Amancia?" Najac asked in a low voice.

"Why is this of your concern?" Amancia demanded.

Najac laughed. "Take it easy, Amancia! I was only going to offer to keep Jocelyn and Marinath while you make your rounds. He read suspicion on her stern face and continued, "Jocelyn really should learn about caring for pigs."

Amancia could not argue this point. "I will bring them when the sun comes up, thank you Najac."

Jocelyn, having been dismissed by Mr. Hermilus, approached excitedly. He was eager to share with Maman the story of the coin, but when he discovered it was cousin Najac with Maman, he contained his enthusiasm. He liked Najac's mirth – unlike Maman and Teti he was always smiling and joking. But Jocelyn also knew this joking often came at the expense of others.

"You will go with Najac tomorrow and learn about caring for his animals," Maman told Jocelyn.

This was too much for the boy who counted the days until he would be viewed as a man and able to earn. "You can count on me, Najac! I will learn well. I will be a great help to you!" he blurted to his cousin.

Najac laughed. "Okay, little man," he rubbed Jocelyn hard on the head. Jocelyn beamed.

As promised, Amancia delivered her two children to Najac after sunup the following morning. Najac spent the morning demonstrating how to get the animals to move, clean them, how to look for disease in them, and many other aspects of pig care young Jocelyn would never have even considered. At midday they went into the family hut to find something small to eat.

As Najac started a fire and put a pot on, Jocelyn perused the unusual objects around him. There were several earthen pots on a high table made crudely of rough wood planks. Jocelyn could not see over the tops of the vessels, so he motioned to Marinath to come over to him, and lifted her up so that she could report on their contents.

When he set her down, she said, "Just water," much more loudly than he had asked his question.

"Hey you kids, leave that *just water* alone, do you understand?" Najac demanded. They were surprised at his suddenly somber voice, and nodded vigorously. After a light-hearted morning with their cousin they were caught off guard, feeling they had done something wrong. Najac sensed this, and motioned them over.

"Here you go, here are mangos for each of you. I have biscuits too that we can have later."

With that, the children felt comforted and let their curiosity return to them as Najac added mysterious ingredients to the pot. They peeled their mangos and watched his every move.

"This is a special meal for the pigs," he explained. Each of these leaves does something different for the pigs' health. This one," he held up a few small, pale green leaves, "keeps infection away. This one," a larger, darker green and shiny leaf, "gives them good poo poos." Jocelyn and Marinath laughed.

"How often do they eat this 'special' meal?" Jocelyn wondered aloud.

"That depends, but usually just a couple times a year we prepare this," Najac said as he generously added several types of grains to the pot. It was beginning to look like a delicious soup to two

29

children who had spent most days hungry. "More this year, though, because many pigs in Haiti are becoming sick. If we don't keep them healthy, the government will come and take them away." Najac seemed to forget he was speaking to children as he grew angry. "I'm not so sure they take them to kill them like they say, though, but are just stealing from the poorest people to have delicious bacon without the work! They say Americans are to blame, but I don't know. I hear America is a good place. A place where nobody is hungry and every child goes to school. You hear different things, and don't know what to believe..." he trailed off, stirring the pot in silence for several moments.

Jocelyn had never heard an adult speak around him in this way. Of course, Najac was only a very young adult, maybe twenty, Jocelyn guessed. To hear Najac speak, Jocelyn pictured the world so much more than what his imagination thought of before. America sounded too good to be true. Maybe one day America would be his *pays étranger*. He wondered if they had delicious soup to eat every day in America, and this made him think of the delicious soup that the pigs would be having when he would probably have no supper now that he had been fed by Najac.

"May I try a taste?" Jocelyn asked timidly. The look on Marinath's face told him she was thinking the same thing.

"This is for the pigs," Najac laughed. "Are you a pig?"

"No, sir, I'm not a pig!" Jocelyn protested.

Marinath was glad not to have asked, seeing how Najac was teasing her brother.

"Oh, food is food, right my friend?" Najac said as he spooned a hearty helping.

This seemed like good reasoning to Jocelyn so he took the wooden spoon from his cousin and blew on the steaming grains until he was confident he would not burn his mouth. Marinath watched expectantly as Jocelyn opened up wide enough to slide the full contents into his little mouth. Even before he closed his mouth over the hot liquid, he was struck with a putrid flavor wholly unfamiliar to him. He fought the instinct to spit it out after Najac had made such a concession to let him sample the soup, and instead gulped the hot mass straight down. Instantly he regretted this decision.

A burning far greater than just the hot temperature traveled down Jocelyn's throat and hit his stomach like an inverted volcano. This was easily read on his face, but as he began dancing around, Najac truly grew amused. He dropped his post at the pot to double over with laughter as his young cousin danced frantically around the room. Jocelyn thought to run out and search for the nearest well, then remembered the 'water' on the table. Despite its impressive weight, he maneuvered one of the pots to the edge and began drinking so vigorously that the fluid spilled carelessly down the front of his skinny frame. The 'water' was only a mild relief to his poor suffering gullet, and quickly Jocelyn gave up on this as well. He started to set the vessel right again when an unfamiliar sensation grabbed hold of him. The room began to spin and he was only barely able to set the earthenware upright and turn back to face Marinath, hoping she had not been as foolish as him. As he turned he fell to the ground, and the room spun even faster.

By this point, Najac was beyond hysterical with laughter. He went to Jocelyn, bent over to grab him by the hands and pull him upright. Jocelyn allowed this momentarily, but once on his feet he bolted out the door. Sunlight hit him like a brick wall, and again he fell straight to the ground. Again and again, he would pick himself up, move in the direction of where he thought the well might be, and dropped again. Marinath did her best to keep up with him and help him, but he behaved so erratically that she grew afraid of him. After several minutes of this, with Najac following behind (his laughter renewed with every fall), Marinath spotted her mother at a distance. She started running toward her and shouting frantically, "Jocelyn is very sick! Jocelyn is very sick!"

Amancia was able to see at a distance how odd her son's behavior was. She gestured for Marinath to head in the direction of the well (Jocelyn *had* been on the right path), shouting, "a bucket of water, child!"

When she reached her son, she grabbed hold of him and shook him. "Amos! Amos!" she barked. "What has happened?!"

Despite her firm grip, Jocelyn fell once and for all into the dry grass beneath them, nearly taking Maman with him. His eyes closed, though she did not know whether it was against the blinding sunlight or he was completely unconscious. She noticed Najac, suddenly silent, slinking back toward the hut, confirming her worst suspicions. She waited an eternity for her daughter to return, then demanded, "Marinath?!"

"Maman, Jocelyn ate the soup for the pigs and it made him sick and he drank Najac's water and now he… he…" Marinath did her best to explain as she rushed over with the bucket, water sloshing over its rugged edges.

"Was this 'water' in an earthenware vessel?" Amancia demanded of her daughter.

Marinath nodded. She handed the bucket to her mother who, planting her feet firmly on the ground, wound back and threw its contents with as much force as possible at her son's face. The desired effect was achieved and Jocelyn began to cough and sputter, and ultimately sit upright. His first memory upon regaining his composure was of the back of his mother storming toward the hut.

"How DARE you hex my son with your wicked Voodoo, Najac!" she screamed. "You are a terrible man! God will see this comes back to you!"

Najac reappeared in the doorway, hoping to get the scene over with. "How was I supposed to know that the soup would make him sick, Amancia? I was never foolish enough to eat it myself. AND, I told Jocelyn and Marinath to *stay away* from the alcohol!" His defense was thin, but he ended with emphasis in hopes of calming his irate cousin down.

Amancia stood for several long moments at a great distance with her hands on her hips, keeping a firm eye on Najac. Najac did not flinch. Marinath wondered if her mother wasn't perhaps cursing Najac for nearly killing her only son. This thought also flickered in Jocelyn's still-woozy mind, and as he stood, he pled with his mother.

"Maman, I'm fine now. I'm fine. God has watched out for me by sending you. And Najac was kind all morning, showing us how to care for the pigs, Maman." For good measure, he held himself as upright as possible, strode the full distance to where Najac stood, and, taking a liberty he never would have with another adult, he punched Najac in the arm. Amancia shifted her focus instantaneously.

"Jocelyn! Don't you DARE strike your cousin!" Amancia moved her hand to her mouth before she could even finish her threat, unsuccessfully covering a wide grin.

"Ha haaaaa," Jocelyn laughed out loud and jumped around. The alcohol consumption had clearly had an impact on him, but his sense of humor was very much intact. Seldom did he get to see his mother so cheered, especially by his misbehavior. Najac rode this roller coaster of emotions with his cousins, ultimately grateful for Jocelyn's interference in his mother's menacing glare – whatever may have been behind it.

As Amancia collected her children and shepherded them home, Marinath remarked, "I don't trust that Najac!"

"You will be smart, both of you, to learn from this. Najac is not a bad man, but you are right, Marinath, he is not to be trusted. If you see someone do bad, then you know that person might do bad to you. You should never do bad because God is watching. But also, others are watching. If you want to be trusted, only let others see you doing good in this world."

These words resonated in each of their minds as the afternoon sun warmed their backs, but none more than Jocelyn's. A headache he hadn't known since a machete was planted in his skull gripped him before they arrived home, and he resolved never to be the cause of another's pain.

Gold from the Well
Jocelyn Apo

VI.   Water

We stay home often. We stay home often by ourselves. A lot of times, my mother may say, it depends, she may say, 'OK, when it get a certain time, go to this person. Tell this person give you some bread and when she come back, Maman will pay you.' Like, I can go to somebody and they can give me a little bread, it's the size of a biscuit, for my dinner. That's how big that thing is, the size of a biscuit. But we'd be satisfied with it. Now, if they give it to us like that, we'd be just fine. But sometimes, we don't get nothing at all. Growing up in my country was not easy. As I was coming up a little guy, I don't know, I can talk to myself. I can feed myself. And as soon as I get big, I can see the difference of what my parents have to go through every day. It was very difficult. I never really communicate with them, ask them questions, you know, what's wrong, when I see them put their hand on their face. And it almost seemed like their body here, but their mind very far away.

One day doing laundry, Amancia noticed that the fish had returned to the creek. She kept this good news to herself, but began quietly collecting reeds. Once partially dry, she stripped the reeds and braided them into a sturdy rope. She searched out three heavy sticks the length of her arm and set to work creating a net which held the three sticks together in a strong triangle, and spanned the space between them with generous slack. She also sought out a sharp stick and split the wood just enough to lodge another piece of rope such that she could spear any caught fish and string them along the reed. Jocelyn remembered the delicious flavor of the fleshy creatures and salivated watching her.

At last the net was ready and, knowing of Marinath's love of the creek, she invited her children to come along.

"You mustn't come too close to Maman!" she advised. "The fish will swim away from your silly games. It occurred to her that this could work to her advantage, so she noted, "but you may play your games far from me and send them into my net, God willing." She proudly held up her clever device.

The three set out joyfully for the creek, celebrating the dinner they would have that night. Jocelyn knew that, unlike most any other food they might come across, the fish must be eaten right away. If Maman was successful, they might lay their heads down with the rare sensation of full bellies. As they arrived at the creek's edge, she halted, rested her net against her knees, and stopped each of her two children by the shoulder, signifying they must stop and pray for a healthful dinner. Jocelyn and Marinath heartily obliged.

With that, they were sent off to play while Amancia positioned herself in thigh-high water where she believed she would be most successful at her task. A rhythm practiced hundreds of times before came back to her, and she deftly plunged an angled side of her net into the water, trapping one or two fish of five or six inches in length at a time. She almost seemed to grow extra limbs in the process of spearing and stringing the caught fish without losing a grip on her net, then repeating the process.

Marinath egged her brother on, believing naively that she might outswim him. She would dive under the water, and at times Jocelyn would be fooled as to what direction she had swum away. She would re-emerge, laughing, when she managed to resurface behind him and take him by surprise. Jocelyn wanted a part in this fun as well.

"Now you chase me, Marinath! You can't catch me!" he teased as he dove under the water. He discovered he could not see well beneath the water, and had to depend on a sense of direction in his head in order to fool her. He certainly did feel the fish swirling about him from time to time, and, wanting to help Maman in her efforts, when he felt a particularly large group he thought to motion to Maman to come to where he was. He stood tall in the water and realized that it was actually quite deep – he was only able to reach his toes to the bottom and have his face above the surface. Surely Marinath had not followed him all this way, and in the blinding sun he made his way back toward the now very small figure that was Maman.

39

Once he was a little more sure of his footing, Jocelyn searched the surface, hoping his opportunity to sneak up on Marinath was not lost. But he could not find her. As he grew closer to Maman, she started.

"Where is your sister?" Then frantic, "WHERE IS YOUR SISTER?!"

Amancia dropped the net and all the fish and raced into the deepest water from where Jocelyn had just returned. She dove beneath the surface several times. By this time Jocelyn felt painfully the urgency of the situation and flailed about, screaming his sister's name.

What seemed an eternity later, Amancia emerged with a limp Marinath. She strode breathlessly to the creek's edge, gasping for Jocelyn to follow. Jocelyn felt only small pangs of relief when he saw his sister in Maman's arms, and knew they must move quickly. Maman found strength from God and broke into a very fast run.

Jocelyn could not keep up with his mother. He reached out to hold her skirt and tripped, crying out. She stopped to wait for him, and slowed her speed to a pace she knew he could match. Without a doubt, their grief delivered them much more quickly to the hut than they ever might have thought possible.

Barely able to speak, Amancia was relieved to discover Teti at home, and, holding their daughter up to him, uttered, "drowned…"

Teti acted instantaneously. To Amancia's shock, he grabbed Marinath's small body by the ankles and held her fully upside down. He began to vigorously dip her, the way Jocelyn had seen Maman dip the laundry in the creek. *Jolt. Jolt. Jolt.* Pause. *Jolt. Jolt. Jolt.* Pause. Water drained all over the dry dirt floor, giving Jocelyn some idea of how nearly perilous Marinath's adventure had been. *Jolt. Jolt. Jolt.* Pause. *Jolt. Jolt. Jolt.* Pause. At last, Marinath began choking. Moving swiftly, Teti righted the poor girl gently, and moved her to his own bed.

As Marinath moaned back into some semblance of consciousness, Amancia fussed over her daughter. She prayed and pled with God for the child's health. Jocelyn recognized exhaustion on his mother's face – he had seen it too many times before. But he stayed silently in a corner the rest of the afternoon, looking on. After some time, he entertained the fleeting thought of his belly full of fish, but checked himself immediately. He would trade a lifetime of full bellies for his sister's life.

* * *

Three days later, things had returned to normal. Amancia would not feel comfortable having the children near the creek for some time, so she left them sleeping in their bed to begin a day of laundry. She whispered a prayer over them and headed out with an unsettled feeling. Amancia tried to quiet her worries by humming a hymn as she walked. She would also resume her collection of reeds to replace the net that some lucky neighbor had happened on the day of the accident.

Jocelyn was the first to stir. He stared up at the ceiling of the hut with faint memories of a pleasant dream. From beside him, he heard the ragged breathing of his sister, whom he thought might be having a bad dream of her own. He casually rolled over to discover that her eyes were rolled back, and she began to shake.

Jocelyn was paralyzed, not knowing what to do. "Maman!..." he began with an impotent voice. He was so terrified he could barely make a sound. "Papa!..."

The pull of two children needing her compelled Amancia to reverse her direction. Though she had no material reason to delay her work, it was not the first, nor hardly the last time in her life she would feel God speaking to her, commanding her to act.

Jocelyn felt that his mother's return was nearly instantaneous. In one giant movement, she lifted him away from his sister and deposited him on her own bed, sweeping then to the table and grabbing garlic cloves from a woven basket. Confident that the stones around the fire were cooled from the intervening days since she last washed laundry, she lifted a flat-bottomed one that fit snugly in the palm of her hand and brought it down mightily on the garlic, finishing with a grinding spin. She repeated this movement once, then gathered up the garlic pieces and moved quickly to her convulsing daughter.

Jocelyn recognized the words Maman's mouth soundlessly made as she held her daughter to her bosom, the garlic to Marinath's nose. "Hail Mary, full of grace. Our Lord is with thee. Blessed art thou among women, and blessed is the fruit of thy womb, Jesus. Holy Mary, Mother of God, pray for us sinners, now and at the hour of our death. Amen."

Marinath went limp in her mother's arms, but Jocelyn knew from the drop of his mother's shoulders that it was a sign of rest. A sign of peace. Maman lay Marinath back down on the bed, and slowly caressed the crushed garlic into the feet of her daughter. Jocelyn marveled at this gesture; he did not question her wisdom.

Amancia became aware of Jocelyn looking on. She knew he would see much harder things in the world, but also knew his young caring heart bled for his sister. "*Croiser les bras*, Jocelyn, we have all lived to see the day," she put simply. He obeyed, thanking God for giving their mother wisdom and sparing the life of his sister.

"She will rest now, Jocelyn," Maman said as she pulled herself together to return to her work. "Be a good brother and watch

43

over her today. When she wakes, and you know she is with you in spirit, go out to old Miss Saraphina. You ask her for a bit of bread. Tell her your sister has been sick, but Maman will pay her tomorrow when the laundry is delivered." Noting that Jocelyn was still in a daze, she demanded harshly of her son, "What did I say, Amos?"

Jocelyn was jolted from his shock by the comfort of his mother's disciplinary tone, and chimed, "When Marinath wakes and is well, ask Miss Saraphina for bread and Maman will pay tomorrow after laundry…" Jocelyn feared he was forgetting something crucial, and searched the room for clues. When his eyes fell on his sister, he added, "And I will be a good brother and I will watch Marinath and pray for her, Maman!"

"You are a good son," Amancia muttered as she left her children and her heart behind, willing her thin legs to push on through the hot grass.

* * *

After my sister was sick, my mother take her to the Voodoo man. She don't take her to the hospital. She take her to the Voodoo man. Just like me, as soon as my sister got into the gate at the Voodoo man, my sister's eyes open. The Voodoo man, he did some type of ceremony. When he doing those type of service like that, 50, 60 people already there. The whole thing full. My sister and I, both of us, drank chicken blood before for the service they done for us. Then the Voodoo man put a big fire in the middle. I mean big fire with charcoal. And he danced right in the big fire. The Voodoo man, he danced in the fire. And then, he tried to make sure everybody join him. So he get my sister, he spin my sister around and my sister fall down right in between the fire. And I guess my sister probably missed her balance or something. She fell down right in the fire. Right in the middle of the fire. She was very little. She fell right in the whole fire. My mouth was wide open. My mother went right in there right quick. God bless my mother. Marinath's stomach was burned. And my sister was very light skinned. Her stomach was burned. The Voodoo man put some medicine on my sister's stomach, and then lay her down. Soon that big piece in her stomach begin to bubble up, bubble up and water and stuff, hurt, she very much full of pain, crying. I'm crying too. She got lot of blisters on her body. But after a while, she got better with no doctor. My sister, Marinath, get to live and have five kids of her own before she pass away.

Gold from the Well
Jocelyn Apo

.

VII.   Leaving

But to go back a little bit, growing up in '60s and '70s, Haiti was going down but it wasn't that bad. But after that, that's why the reason why my mom would give me away to somebody who can feed me better. She was very concerned. I was kind of young to really learn exactly what's really going on in the country. But I can watch my own family and cannot feed us. And I watched them try to figure out what we're gonna eat today. And one important thing about my Maman today, and I always talking to her and tell her thank you for all she have done for me. She always told me to appreciate no matter what, to appreciate. And she always told me when somebody did wrong to you, always pray for nothing bad to happen to them. She always give me the tools I need. When I become adult one day, I can go through life without a problem.

"Amos, you remember when you were a small boy and grown men would trust you? Remember Mr. Hermilus asked you to hold money for him?" Amancia asked her son whom, at 12 years of age, was wiry but growing taller every day.

Jocelyn would NEVER forget the honor of Mr. Hermilus asking him to hold money for him. It was weeks longer than what the gentleman had said it would be before he came to their humble hut to reclaim his small treasure, so he was truly impressed with the boy, though rewarded him only with his praise. Or so Jocelyn had thought.

"I remember, Maman!" he reminisced.

"Mr. Hermilus is a friend to Dessalines Casseus. Mr. Casseus is another man who owns land," Maman began with hesitation in her voice. She paused and turned away from Jocelyn to stoke her fire.

Jocelyn waited patiently, but the excitement of playing a role in the lives of these men gave him a restless energy. He picked up a stone and tossed it back and forth between dusty hands.

"You will go live with Mr. Casseus and work on his farm," Maman said quietly and simply.

"I will?!" The stone dropped between his feet. He clasped his hands together and ran to Maman. His height matched hers now and while he knew not to disturb her at the fire, he hung an arm around one of her thin shoulders and laid his head on the opposite one. She still did not face him.

"Yes, God has given you an opportunity to work, Amos, and you will eat every single day at Mr. Casseus's home. You will have a place to sleep, you will learn, and you will receive your confirmation if you work hard as I have taught you." Amancia stirred the laundry in the pot, staring absently into the boiling water.

Uncharacteristically, she then turned and looked straight into her son's eyes. He reflexively looked down until she grabbed his chin, pulling it upward, signaling that he was to meet her gaze. "In all that you do, Amos, I want you to remember always. Pray as though it is all up to God. But WORK as though it is all up to you." Jocelyn had no memory of his mother's eyes glistening as they did just then, though he remembered these words from the many times she had shared them before. He placed his head on her shoulder and vowed to make her proud. He then broke away and danced around the room, celebrating this venture into manhood and a life-long dedication to hard work.

* * *

In the days that followed, Amancia and Teti did their best to prepare Jocelyn for his work and being away. Papa Teti presented Jocelyn with a burlap shirt and pants that had been his, knowing that the Casseus family would expect him to be dressed each day. Maman had to braid a new belt that could cinch in the pants as Jocelyn's thin frame swum inside the pants of his father, though he too was a very thin man.

As she admired her work, Maman mused in a quiet voice, "Your Papa Teti has been so good to you, considering…"

Jocelyn waited for her to finish. He learned very young not to press Maman. Never to question. But in this case she never

49

completed her sentence, and he committed the exchange to memory. Something weighed on her but his sheltered adolescent mind could not fully grasp what it was.

She sighed heavily. "Tomorrow he will bring you to Mr. Casseus where you will stay until he no longer needs you. I say until he no longer needs you because you will give him absolutely NO reason to send you back, is that very clear, young man?"

"Of course, Maman! I will work hard! I will work SO hard!" her Amos replied emphatically.

"It's not just about hard work, Amos. You must 'get along', do you understand?"

"I get along with everyone, Maman!" Jocelyn answered innocently. He knew that his happy manner pleased everyone.

"I mean that even if someone crosses you, or accuses you of something wrongly, or behaves in an unchristian way toward you, you must turn the other cheek. Remember, God hands out the ultimate reward, and he will want you to turn the other cheek. This does not mean you let others strike you down. Only God can kill you. Only God can kill me. But in small ways – you will come to understand exactly what I mean – do not deny, do not contradict, and do not falsely admit to wrong. Simply say, 'I'm sorry you are upset. 'I will always do my best for you.' Do you understand?"

Jocelyn's small life had given him little context for his mother's words, but as he always did when she was making a point of imparting wisdom, he carved her words into his memory, and worked to attach them to feelings of loss, embarrassment, rejection so that he could retrieve them if his new job ever made him low.

Amancia prepared a special dinner, making trades on promise with cousin Najac for bits of pork and grains. That evening she instructed Jocelyn and Marinath, as always, to *croiser les bras*, and thank God for work. She then added her gratitude for a prosperous future. Jocelyn reflected that his mother almost never spoke of it, yet he *always* thought of the future. She wedged herself between the children in their bed, and embraced them as they fell asleep.

* * *

Goodbyes the next morning were very emotional. Jocelyn had been so focused on his opportunity that, although he had given thought to how much he would miss his family, not until he was setting off on foot with Papa Teti to town (where Mr. Casseus would pick him up in a truck) had he considered how long it would be before he saw them all again.

"Be a good worker and be brave, Amos my son," Maman spoke softly into his ear as she embraced him, fighting her impulse not to let go. "What else does Maman tell you?"

Jocelyn, filled with ambivalence, dutifully responded, "Thank

God every day for all he gives me. Pray like it is all up to Him, but work like it is all up to me."

"Yes, son, that's it," she held him a few moments longer. Jocelyn caught sight of Marinath, kicking a stone through the grass, visibly sad for losing her playmate. He subtly gestured to Maman, then broke away to comfort her. He summoned that part of himself intent on coaxing a smile from everyone, quickly went over to her and popped upside down onto his head. "Whatcha lookin' at down here, little sister?" he asked in the most casual tone he could, despite his ridiculous appearance. His silliness garnered the laughter he had hoped it would. She burst out laughing and could not resist pushing him backwards by his skinny legs.

"AAArrrrggghhhh," Jocelyn exaggerated his fall, bringing even more laughter from Marinath's beautiful face. She covered her mouth when she caught Maman's watchful eye, but then Maman quietly retracted her admonition by touching Marinath's arm as she walked back to the house.

Maman glanced back over her shoulder to see her young son brushing himself off, still wearing his trademark smile. He looked over to see her eyes glistening once again – so rare a sight. Now it was Jocelyn's turn to fight the urge to run back to her; instead, he tipped his head to his Maman, turned to Papa Teti and said, "Okay, let's go." As he walked past Marinath, who was looking away in her own struggle, he jolted her off balance with a push from his hip. It was too much. Her sudden laugh soon bore sobs as Jocelyn quickened his pace down the road.

Jocelyn and Papa Teti walked in silence to town. Jocelyn turned over in his mind his mother's remark in the days before about Papa Teti being a good father to him "considering…" Jocelyn knew that Papa Teti was not Yenocen's father, but Papa did nice things for Yenocen from time to time before Yenocen died. Were there different kinds of fathers, Jocelyn wondered. But 'what made a father?' he asked himself. Papa put food in their bellies. He taught him many things. And he knew Papa Teti cared very much for him.

"Papa," Jocelyn said when they were very nearly to the meeting point, though they were well ahead of the midday meeting time Mr. Casseus had designated, in order to guard against a bad start with his new employer.

"Mmmm?" Papa responded, eyes set on the road ahead of them.

Jocelyn chose his words carefully. "Papa, you have been a very good Papa. I thank God for you."

If Papa Teti gleaned any of Jocelyn's hidden meaning, he did not let on. Almost without any visible reaction, he merely placed his hand on the boy's shoulder, only slightly below his own now, but did not shift his gaze. "Thank you, Jocelyn. Thank you, son," he quietly answered.

They continued into town, and enjoyed a final math lesson as they nervously awaited the arrival of Mr. Casseus. At last, a dust-covered, faded green truck bounced along the road to where they were. Papa and Jocelyn both scrambled to their feet.

A very tall man who had many other outward signs of good nutrition emerged from the driver's seat and walked around to greet the two Apo men. He stood with his arms folded while Papa Teti attempted a less embarrassing goodbye than had taken place at home. For the stranger's sake, he brought his strong hand down very firmly on Jocelyn's shoulder, raised the boy's chin with his other hand, and said simply, "You will be missed. Show Mr. Casseus what a good worker you are."

Jocelyn met his eyes for a flicker and nodded. He blinked vigorously in a naïve attempt to fan away the tears pushing themselves out of his large brown eyes. Believing he might have been successful, he turned to face Mr. Casseus, saying cheerfully, "Thank you, Mr. Casseus, for this opportunity. I will work very hard for you."

Dessalines Casseus, who had spoken no words to this point, shook Papa Teti's hand and said plainly, "you ride in the back there, boy," and he walked back around to the driver's seat. Papa comforted himself that Amancia had heard Dessalines would be a fair man. But as the boy wiped his eyes and stared back at him from the bed of the truck, Papa's heart sunk.

* * *

"This is my *family's* home," Mr. Casseus pointed out roughly as he took Jocelyn around his property. Jocelyn knew from the harsh tone Mr. Casseus used for the word 'family' that he would never be considered among them.

"I have four children. My son, Walken is grown, and my daughter Leila is nearly so. Odney is about your age and you will work with him a great deal. Ana is the baby," he shot Jocelyn a look reminding him again of his position. Jocelyn looked instantly to the ground.

Jocelyn deigned to raise his eyes and admire the family home. The numerous structures did not quite have the integrity of the shops in town, but he noted that the walls had been reinforced with stucco. From a concrete slab at the doorway, Jocelyn could tell that the parents' small cottage boasted a real floor and metal roof. A small cottage for the children was of similar design without the concrete floor. A kitchen was also free-standing, large enough for a great deal of cooking to be done, a generous supply of charcoal to be housed for this purpose, and plenty of space for the mother and children to be

55

fed. But only Mr. Casseus sat at table to dine; within the cottage he shared with his wife, a small desk-sized table stood, and his meals were elaborately laid there for the proverbial lord of the manor, Jocelyn would later discover.

Not one but TWO outhouses were positioned away from each of the bedroom buildings. Jocelyn recognized the great luxury in this feature, but Mr. Casseus was quick to point out that he knew Jocelyn had grown up without going in an outhouse, and he would be expected to go far out in the fields like the animals, and dig a hole. It was clear that Mr. Casseus did not consider this an offense since it was nothing new for Jocelyn, so Jocelyn accepted this in the matter-of-fact manner presented to him. Finally, Mr. Casseus brought him around to a structure not unlike Jocelyn's own home, but even smaller.

"This is where you will sleep by yourself," Mr. Casseus noted. There was a small mattress almost as nice as the one Jocelyn's parents slept on. He began to recognize the small ways that he would be coming up in the world, especially when Mr. Casseus put in, "you will NOT eat in here if you want to avoid vermin. And you will share this room if we hire other help, do you understand?"

Jocelyn was so focused on the "eat" aspect of this statement that he respectfully, even joyfully answered, "Yes sir, Mr. Casseus. I will care for this beautiful room like it was my own home. I thank you for this opportunity, and I thank God he has sent you into my life!"

Mr. Casseus was embarrassed for this boy's outpouring, gave him a patronizing pat on the shoulder and muttered impatiently, "okay, okay, that's fine boy."

Without further ado, Jocelyn was put straight to work bringing water from the well to the kitchen, shucking dry corn for the chickens, then helping Odney feed the chickens, calling them with a gentle, throbbing whistle. This subtle sound brought flocks and flocks swarming into the compound, badly startling Jocelyn. He thought of his mother's advice to get along, so after having introducing himself perhaps a little too cheerfully to the boss's son, he made use of this opportunity to poke fun at himself.

"I'm the biggest chicken here, maybe," he joked, artfully conveying to this young man who stood several inches shorter than himself that he, Jocelyn, would defer to Odney's authority. When Odney directed him to a basin with water outside the kitchen where they washed their hands, and then was told to wait outside the building and food would be brought to him, Jocelyn interpreted this as success in forging their relationship.

After a long wait, during which he heard conversation and laughter of the family inside, the maid emerged with a tray containing a plate generously heaped with food. Jocelyn thought his eyes might pop out of his head at this display which could not possibly be meant for him! Indeed it was not, and the maid set a determined course for the parents' cottage. Still, it gave him hope of laying his head on his new, luxurious mattress with a full belly that night.

After the maid's return, there was another ten minutes of bustling inside the kitchen. Jocelyn had been inside to deliver the water, so he knew there was not a table for the family. He wondered if they would emerge with their meals, but they did not. In time, however, the maid brought him a cabbage leaf heaped with mais mouline and a strip of brown meat he presumed to be chicken, considering his surroundings. Although the look on the maid's face was almost apologetic with this small presentation, Jocelyn eagerly took it into his left hand and burst out with an enthusiastic, "Thank you!!!!" As soon as she turned, he made the sign of the cross with his free hand and thanked God for so generous a dinner. But just as he was about to take a bite, he thought of Maman and Marinath and what they might be eating for her dinner that night. He crossed himself again.

"Dear God, please also look out for my family and give them food to eat. Thank you for my family and thank you for the opportunity to work. It has already brought me such treasure." With that, though thoughts of his family could not be entirely dispelled, he popped this small piece of meat into his mouth and savored his first taste of chicken.

* * *

They put me to sleep in something that looked like a shed and it's in the yard. That's where I would be sleeping. Alone. And sometimes I got scared. Yes. And sometimes, in the middle of the night, I cry. I miss my mom. Sometimes, I wanna get up to go take a pee-pee, and I feel like somebody outside, even though their whole yard is fenced. Not fence like a fence here. They have a type of fence, but you know, people can still come in. But this fence, every corner is left wide open. Sometimes, if it's raining pretty heavy and this shed got a hole in it and I'm kind of wet or something, if I ask the person I live with, 'Can I sleep in one of the house where the other people sleep,' and they would tell me yes. And no problem, I go over there. I go sleep. But otherwise, they prefer me to sleep over there in the shed. And sometimes, I feel like somebody outside. I don't want to get up and go use bathroom. Because we don't have anything to use inside, we gotta go outside, pee outside. It was very difficult and it was kind of tough. Sometimes I pee pee in the bed because I so scared. It was one time they need a lot of help. So there was another boy from another city in Haiti come and work with them and he was living there. While he was living there, him and I was sleeping together. Sometimes when I wanna go use bathroom at night, I call him to go with me. But he's sleeping so good, he doesn't wanna go.

59

But mostly I in the shed alone and I don't wanna go outside to pee pee, it's too dark. There's no light outside. No nothing. You know, if I wasn't tired yet, look like when I go to bed, I wasn't gonna sleep at all because I cannot bring my body to a level it needs to be to go to sleep because it was simply too difficult. Sometimes, you need somebody to comfort you or you need something to talk about, you need something to look to, so you can go for a sleep. But you know, you're by yourself. You go in the room by yourself. You do this by yourself. And I don't get used to this stuff. I left my Maman. Another time, when they feed me good, they give me plenty of food I eat. And I was very emotional, too, because I've been thinking about my mother. The reason why she gave me away, so somebody can take care of me. I'm eating good here and I'm thinking about my mom, she probably cannot eat. That was bringing me down, too. I think about her a lot. And she give me away so I can have a better life. And then, so I can eat good. That's why she gave me away. But I had never have a thought that she didn't love me. Never thinking like that. I always thinking she loves me.

VIII. Work

So, this family, thanks to my Maman, thanks to God, I stay with them for quite some time. I stay with them, I believe I went over there when I was like 13. And then I leave over there maybe 16 or 17. So every day, for a good amount of time while I live with them, I gotta look for the North Star because I don't have a radio. I don't have a TV. I don't have a watch. I have to get up in a good amount of time. I have to watch the North Star. The North Star tell me when to get up. If I get up, I'm confused. And for some reason, sometimes, it's very difficult for me to bring myself where I'm supposed to be. Sometimes, most of the time, the North Star helped me a lot. When I come in, I go sit outside. I get up in the middle of sleep. Every time I wake up, I look at the North Star. If it is very high in the sky, I go back to bed. If it's low, down flush where it's supposed to be, and then I get up and go. That's how I do it for many years. And then a lot of times, too, I listen to rooster. Rooster, and they're singing. They're singing more often when it's time, morning, for people to get up. When it's time for morning. Yes, the rooster make a lot of noise. Coo-coo-a-la-coo.

For four years, almost every day was the same for Jocelyn – seven days a week. He would watch for the North Star. When it approached the horizon, it was time to rise. In time, his body grew

61

more accustomed to knowing this time on its own, but in the beginning he spent many restless nights worried he would oversleep.

Once he rose, he would walk a great distance to milk the cow, as Mr. Casseus had taught him on his second day. He would lead the cows to a fresh area to graze, make sure they were well secured, then walk the great distance back to deliver milk to the family. He would be given a small morning meal. About the time that he ate, the chickens ate too. Without prompting, flocks of them descended from the trees overhead, and Jocelyn and Odney spread the morning corn quickly.

Next, Jocelyn would go to the well and wash himself with just a bucket of water and his hands. Though his work throughout the day left him dirty for bed, it was more important that he be clean for catechism.

At 8:00 a.m. he would report for catechism at a small church a long walk from the farm, except on Sunday, when he was permitted to attend mass. Jocelyn treasured this part of his day the most. The priest taught him about the Bible, Jesus's gift to mankind, and God's will for His people. Jocelyn had gotten no better at sitting still than he had been for his brief time as a student in school, and this was his only obstacle to fully embracing the experience. But thinking of his Maman, and how proud she would be to know he was preparing for his First Communion helped him quiet his twirling feet, his fidgety hands. He also learned to bargain with God. He felt God's warm love toward him, and believed that since God had made him an active boy, suited well for work, He could forgive Jocelyn for his busy limbs in a house of worship.

Jocelyn would work on the farm until just before the sun went down. Walking the two miles back to where the cows were tethered and the fields lay, he was given all types of work, depending on the day. Most assuredly, digging in the dirt would be involved. Many days, he would carefully remove the suckers from banana trees and give them a new home in the soil where they would grow to be new trees. By hand, he planted rows of corn in the spring and harvested it in the late summer. Jocelyn learned to watch the leaves on the bean plants, and pull them just as they turned yellow. He was taught when to cut the rice, pull the yams, replant yucca. Most days he had a piece of fruit or a vegetable in a sack that he could enjoy when he got hungry midday. On the hottest days when he could not be working near a well, he remembered the trick from his childhood of placing a stone in his parched mouth to alleviate miserable thirst.

Jocelyn returned to the home site in time to feed the chickens again, then watch them ascend of their own volition back into the tree branches above for the night. Mealtime in the evening differed very little from his first meal on the Casseus farm. Though Jocelyn continued to grow, and his back-breaking labors increased his appetite immensely, he never again knew true hunger when he laid his head down at night while in the care of the Casseus family.

IX.   Dream

*One day I have a dream. I was at a well. We call it, "Puits".
This thing is very deep. Got water in it. That's where we get the water
to cook, to drink. Then one day I have a dream. I'm pulling and,
what's coming up? MONEY. I don't say anything. To my mother, to
anybody. I keep it to myself. That was my dream that my life going to
have something for me, that it will change. When I have a dream that I
was anywhere and pull up something that looked like water, but really,
I was pulling up money. Money, that was my dream, God gave to me
and blessed me, blessed my heart. And all my family warned me that I
was dreaming that one day my life was gonna be good. And it continue
to be good. Because when I had those dreams when I was very, very
young, I would never thought in my whole entire family I was the
special one. And I was the ugliest, too. Everybody was better looking
than I am. Everybody. And so, some of those kids sometimes, they used
to call me ugly. And when I catch them call me ugly, I don't wanna
fight them because I don't want them to beat me up. And I call my
mother and I tell my mother who said that to me, and my mom would
give them a dirty look. And then I feel better, then I go back to school.
But that dream about the well? That told me my life was going to be
something special. God make my life special. I wake up SO happy!
Then, I was having that dream very often. Even today, I still have that
feeling. Not as much as dream as much as I have before, but every*

once in a while. I know one day I'm gonna get there. And I know it's coming. And I have patience. I'm not in a hurry. But before I die, I know something is coming. I just don't know what it is.

X.   Communion

When you get your First Communion, they do a lot of celebration for you and that was the first time I sat at a table to eat. And I ate good that day. Yes, in 1975, that's when I received my First Communion on July 13, 1975. And that was the first time, too, at age 15, I have my first pair of shoes. It was so good.

Jocelyn was not in the practice of following a calendar or thinking about the passage of time. The Haitian seasons did not change much, except that the summers were rainier. In this way, Jocelyn knew he had spent two years away from his family, and that he had received all his catechism and was ready for his First Communion.

Dessalines had developed an affection for Jocelyn and his work ethic, even if the threat of corporal punishment loomed over the boy at any given moment. Wetting the bed because of a fear of going outside on pitch black cloudy nights (which actually *had* bought him several spankings with a stick), or 'borrowing' a neglected bicycle to teach himself to ride were just two examples of behaviors Jocelyn knew, or feared, would displease his employer and cost him a whipping or, worse, being sent home. In this latter case, when Mr. Casseus discovered him holding himself up along the kitchen wall while he pedaled the rickety contraption (whose tires had long since been removed), Jocelyn believed he was surely in for a pain that would make mounting the seat again impossible. Instead, Mr. Casseus was impressed with Jocelyn's initiative and skill on mere metal rims, and offered him the bicycle for transporting himself around the farm. Jocelyn's amazement was almost unprecedented.

Likewise, it was a beautiful surprise to the boy when Mr. Casseus approached him one Sunday after mass.

"Father Suffrard has shared that you are ready to take communion," he said, placing a hand on Jocelyn's shoulder.

"Yes." Jocelyn replied joyfully. "God bless me, the good Father told me so."

"We will celebrate," Mr. Casseus said very simply. Jocelyn was jumping up and down inside at the idea that *he* would be at the center of *any* celebration. That it was to take God's sacrament for the first time made it all the more magical.

A few days later, he was held back from going to church when the shoemaker came to the farm. Jocelyn's invitation into the Casseus cottage was, itself, a rare treat. But the prospect of owning his own shoes was even more magnificent. The shoemaker instructed Jocelyn to lift his foot. Using a rough string, the man lay one piece on the floor and instructed Jocelyn to step on it with the length of his foot.

Then he made notes. He did this again with a new piece of string crossing the widest part of his foot. The man made more notes and conferred with Mr. Casseus before leaving. Jocelyn was unceremoniously returned to the fields, and life resumed, though Jocelyn carried this new little piece of excitement with him everywhere.

The following week, the shoemaker returned with Jocelyn's shoes. He was, again, invited into the cottage to be fitted properly. When Jocelyn saw the crisp leather shoes sewn just to his size, he became embarrassed for the dirtiness of his feet. But clearly the shoemaker was accustomed to a clientele not unlike Jocelyn whose feet bore the unmistakable signs of having spent a lifetime uncovered, so he very simply coaxed the boy over and helped him into the shoes.

Jocelyn realized that he didn't know *what* exactly he was expecting, but it was not this. His feet seemed to argue with him about the need for shoes. He followed the instruction to walk around the room, and only felt awkward and uncomfortable. All the wealthy men he had seen in his life walked effortlessly in shoes. Yet this experience was even more foreign to him than learning to ride the tireless bicycle. Still, Jocelyn knew better than to complain.

"What do you think, boy?" Mr. Casseus demanded, looking on.

"Oh, thank you very much for this generous gift, Mr. Casseus!" One of Jocelyn's bargains with God was to avoid a lie whenever possible. "I can't believe I am so lucky to have an employer who would go to this trouble for me. For my First Communion," he added enthusiastically. All true.

Mr. Casseus beamed. "Take care of those shoes, boy! But take them to your hut and practice walking in them when your feet are *clean*. And don't ever wear them in the fields – they are for church on Sundays only!"

Jocelyn was actually relieved that he would not be expected to wear these shoes always, and, moreover, that it was not obvious to Mr. Casseus how clumsy he felt. Jocelyn never wanted for it to appear that any nicety was above him.

"Yes sir!" Jocelyn responded, happily removing the beautiful shoes. For good measure, he cradled them like a baby in his arms, asked to be dismissed, and laid the shoes in the corner of his hut that he knew to stay driest whatever the weather.

The following Saturday night, when his work was done and his evening meal eaten, Jocelyn stayed up late to wash the clothes he wore every day. He wrung and shook the water from them as best he could, and folded them as his mother had taught him and placed them under the mattress. Jocelyn lamented that he could not let them dry for two nights as they would need to, but having only one set of clothes, there was really no choice in the matter. He would take extra care milking in the morning (hopefully the cows would not choose this as one of many days when they kicked him) and if the rain held off, the walk there and back would be ample time for his clothes to finish drying.

The following morning, it was as though God had answered his prayers for this vision. After washing up, Jocelyn was quite presentable for the morning meal in his clean, pressed burlap clothes and new shoes. He had practiced religiously every night, washing his feet before he retired for the evening. His gate was nowhere near *natural*, per se, but he had at least learned to walk in them without appearing to be in pain.

When the family arrived at the church, Jocelyn was sent to the front with two other neighboring peasant boys to take their First Communion together. Very little was made of the event as regarded the congregation, however the specialness was felt keenly by Jocelyn when Father Suffrard held the wafer over his young, eager face, declaring, 'the body of Christ.' Jocelyn blinked tears away as he accepted the perfect white circle. He closed his eyes and shared a brief private moment with God and his family – there only in spirit – and opened them again as Father made the sign of the cross over him, then patted Jocelyn affectionately on the head. Jocelyn knew he was made bigger, stronger and more mature by the body of Christ, and looked forward to a future in Jesus's warm embrace.

When the family returned to the homestead, Jocelyn received *Mr. Casseus's* usual treatment. It was almost too much for the humble boy to absorb. He was sat at the small table in the cottage and served a midday meal consisting of equal parts meat, rice, vegetables, and sweet corn bread. A warm cup of coffee with store bought sugar was served to him, though he was unsure of this dark beverage that would grow to be his best friend as an adult. When he rose from the table, he respectfully extended his profuse thanks to all members of the family and help that remained in the vicinity.

As he walked outside, Mr. Casseus followed him, placing a hand on the boy's shoulder.

"You're getting big now, Jocelyn. You eat a lot of food. It's time for you to get a job," Mr. Casseus said, gesturing with his head back to cottage, in recognition of the large meal he had just consumed. "So I am going to pay you a salary for the days when your labor is the hardest. Do you understand?"

Of course Jocelyn understood the words Mr. Casseus was speaking, but wasn't sure what all lay within them. He chose to take this as a compliment, of course, and recognition that Jocelyn probably *could* go elsewhere and earn a true salary in lieu of modest room and board.

"Thank you, Mr. Casseus!" Jocelyn chimed, genuinely grateful for all the rites of passage that Mr. Casseus had facilitated in the span of only a couple weeks. At his own insistence, he rode out to the fields (shoeless) to be of help for the remainder of the afternoon, whistling with the joy that only a truly full belly imparts.

Gold from the Well
Jocelyn Apo

XI. Revelation

It was a celebration on my father's side, my real father's side, no boy.
Just me. They were celebrating that I was coming as a boy. My
sisters on my father side, they come to me because I was kinda shy.
They come to me, say hi, they let me know I am their brother, and I
make my head down and keep going. My real father sister always
embrace me. I swear to God, she always say, "That's your father.
That's your father." Every time she say that, I always laugh and I
run away. That's the only time I heard from somebody. My mom
never said nothing. My stepdad never said nothing. I learn a little
bit. Then a little bit. Then a little bit.

Jocelyn was like a new boy. A man. Catechism was over, and
he had demonstrated his prowess on the tireless bicycle so adeptly
that he was often sent on errands in town in the mornings before
working the fields.

One hot day, he rode his bicycle into town, gripping a small
drawstring bag bearing more money than he had ever seen personally.
This was not to say it was a large sum of money, only that having a
role in commerce was entirely new to Jocelyn, and he was thoroughly
invigorated by the escapade.

Soon, though, as he passed pedestrians on their way *out* of town, he could tell from the looks on their faces that he was projecting too obvious a joy. Any other day, Jocelyn was happy to project joy in the world, but because he was charged with protecting Mr. Casseus's money, and exchanging it for coffee beans, he quickly realized how important it would be to keep a low profile. He checked himself, focused his efforts on pulling in the corners of his smile and directing his attention on the dry goods store.

Believing he had succeeded in this effort, Jocelyn was then thrown off his mental balance (only barely keeping physical balance) when an older woman with two young and pretty women, stared at him, agape. They stopped in their footsteps along the road, and he was soon powerless to keep the bicycle upright. As gracefully as he could, he stopped and dismounted, making every effort to make the action appear purposeful. He gripped the sweaty bag between his palm and the handlebars, and fought the urge to turn and face these women whose stares still held his whole being hostage.

"Jocelyn Apo?!" the older woman cried out with delight. Now Jocelyn truly *was* unable to keep his focus on the shop. '*Of course!*' he thought to himself. He must know these women from his childhood. A certain familiarity was undeniable. Still, he had no solid memory of any of them.

"Oui?" Jocelyn replied politely, turning to face them and allowing his smile to resume its very comfortable home across his broad face. His mother's tales of Voodoo, and his nervousness over his prized errand began to leave him.

The older woman approached him gingerly. Despite her outburst, she now seemed speechless. He was, likewise, unsure what to say.

"Jocelyn Apo!" She clicked her tongue repeatedly. "Jocelyn, you are a special boy, Jocelyn. Do you know it? A special boy. A special boy to ME, Jocelyn. Do you know who I am?"

Jocelyn simply shook his head, but tried to maintain a polite smile.

"These are your SISTERS, Jocelyn!" the woman asserted.

Jocelyn surveyed the girls. He had not had the pleasure of seeing his beloved Marinath for almost a year when he last paid a visit, but he was confident that neither of these young women was her. His confusion was palpable, so the older woman relieved him.

"Go on your way, Jocelyn. You'll meet your father soon, I am sure!" and with that she gave the growing boy an awkward hug. Jocelyn did his best to be polite, but gripped the handlebars of his odd-looking bicycle and ran off. This was not the first time he believed he had encountered madness in a person, and he knew it would not be his last.

But as he moved through his errand, and the rest of his day, Jocelyn worked at holding this strange encounter up against all he remembered to be true. In his collection of wisdom and memories of his Maman, his childhood, a portrait of the truth was beginning to suggest itself. He lay his head down on his mattress and spoke aloud to the roommate he was lucky enough to be enjoying for a brief time.

"Tell me about your family, Wilkens," Jocelyn mused, staring at the ceiling of their pleasantly warm hut.

"Sure! What do you want to know about my family?" Wilkens responded. The younger boy was more recently separated and seemed delighted to reminisce.

"Just... tell me something!" Jocelyn put in wistfully.

Wilkens launched into great memories of his three brothers and, apparently, *very* bossy oldest sister.

"All one daddy?" Jocelyn asked casually.

"No. No. Five kids, one daddy? No. My bossy sister has a different daddy and we tease her about that. He is SO ugly!" Wilkens laughed out loud. "I think my youngest brother has a different daddy too, but he doesn't bother us, so we don't say anything," Wilkens put in, matter-of-factly.

Jocelyn went to sleep with this idea turning over in his head. In truth, his mother had pointed out through his entire childhood that somehow Jocelyn was particularly blessed to have the love and care of his father, Papa Teti. Jocelyn knew for certain *he* could love no man as he loved Papa.

At least once a week, Jocelyn found himself in town, and every few of these times, he would encounter the older woman and/or one (or both) of the younger two. These beautiful women also insisted to him that they were his sisters. Finally, one fateful day, his apparent aunt pointed down the dusty road, far into the distance.

"There is your father!" she declared. "My brother, Hachacha. Hachacha Ojasma. Jocelyn squinted his eyes, and saw a man, short, dark-skinned like himself. He could not make out the man's face at all, but looked back into the woman's eyes and, in that moment, knew it to be true. He nodded gratefully to his aunt, recognizing that she had no malice in wanting them to meet. In slow motion he mounted his feeble bicycle and rode mechanically toward the man, who had just been strolling casually down the road. Jocelyn grew horribly nervous, not having the first idea what he would say to Hachacha. He was gripped by thoughts of Papa Teti. Papa was such a good man, he would understand, but it was still not a comfortable thought for

Jocelyn. Without warning, the man entered a place unknown to Jocelyn – maybe a place to drink alcohol. Jocelyn took this as a sign from God that they should not meet that day. But the desire to meet Hachacha *some* day planted itself in his heart and began to grow.

XII. Conflict

And one day he got so angry with me, unnecessary. He said let's fight.
He told me, 'let's fight.' And then, we start fighting. Lucky for me, I hit
him. Now, we're talking about a grown man. Yes. We fight. When we
fight, the fight probably last maybe, probably, one or two minutes.
Lucky for me, God bless me, I hit him above his eye. And then, he hit
me and knocked me out. And then, when I get up, I follow him. I was
crying. I cried very bad. I tell him, I said, 'Why you doing this? I don't
do anything to you. Why you doing this? I don't do anything. Why you
doing this? I don't do anything. Why you don't like me? I don't do
anything.' I keep saying that to him. And he turned around, he said to
me, 'If you gonna be here, I'm not gonna be here.' So it's not a way,
whether for him to be there, I have to be out of there.

Jocelyn enjoyed the shift in compensation at the Casseus farm.
He was assigned the clearing of an enormous strip of weeds along the
sugarcane field. Even when he did not have the proper tools, Mr.
Casseus gave Jocelyn use of his own, *and* paid the young man in cash.
Jocelyn's solitary goal was to save his money, and only use it smartly,
or get it to his Maman, but only if he could be VERY sure she would
receive it. About once a year he was given the full day off that it took
for him to go home to her and return. How delighted she was when
her 16-year-old son made his surprise pilgrimage bearing enough

money to feed the household for a month! Maman urged Jocelyn to find a smart use of his money – one that would yield more. He set his young mind working.

One day soon after when he was in town on his bicycle, he discovered a man at the side of the road selling a young bull. The man was asking three dollars for the bull, which seemed a fair price to Jocelyn. He had cared for cows for a few years now and knew the signs of illness; he saw none in this fine animal. So, juggling one side of the handlebars in one hand and the rope tether in the other, he fumbled his way back to the farm, $3 poorer. He added the bull to the herd with Mr. Casseus's permission, but the young bull received much more of Jocelyn's *affection* than his other charges.

Some months later, Jocelyn had worked and saved 25 dollars. TWENTY-FIVE dollars! Papa's math lessons stuck firmly with him, and he knew 25 was a significant number. On a pass through town, another man was selling a beautiful young adult female cow which he claimed was carrying a calf. Jocelyn was excited at the idea of starting his own herd of cows, but did not have the $30 this man was asking. This was a high price, indeed, but a good investment because a female could keep making more cows. His mind again set to work.

"What if I give you twenty-five dollars *and* a healthy young bull this big?" Jocelyn asked the farmer, holding his hand up to his own breastbone.

82

The farmer made such a good show of dismissing the idea that Jocelyn hung his head and walked away. The farmer scrambled to recover.

"How well has this bull been cared for?" he questioned suspiciously.

"So well that I don't *really* want to give him up!" Jocelyn replied quite honestly. He went into great detail about how he coaxed the bull to eat and drink, and how much he had grown in the months he owned it.

"Okay, okay," the farmer conceded. You bring this bull tomorrow, and your twenty-five dollars, and if he is as healthy as you say, we make a deal."

Jocelyn considered this. He had no way of knowing if the man would have been willing to come down on his price, but he liked to believe that he was effectively reaping a $2 return on his investment already. He agreed to make the deal, returned the next day for the exchange, and stifled his emotions as walked away from his prized bull.

When Jocelyn returned to the farm, Mr. Casseus was out in the fields showing a young man in his mid 20s around. The two approached him.

"What have you here, Jocelyn?" Mr. Casseus inquired with great interest.

Jocelyn beamed. "Ah, Mr. Casseus, I have saved the money you have generously paid me for my work. This cow is going to have a baby. I traded my bull and some cash for her because I know she will make more babies! I hope that's okay, and when the baby gets big I will take it to my Maman so it does not take any more food from the other cows!" Jocelyn had not considered that this trade would lead to asking Mr. Casseus to feed *two* cows on his property, so he was glad he thought of this bit about Maman at the last moment.

"Very resourceful, Jocelyn," Mr. Casseus praised him. "I see I have taught you well. Jocelyn, I want you to meet Mr. Delcine. He will be a manager on the property, and you will now go to him for your work, do you understand?"

Jocelyn felt confident in this introduction because Mr. Casseus had been so kind to him in front of the stranger. Still, Jocelyn deferentially looked at the ground and quietly said to Mr. Delcine, "I will work very hard for you, Mr. Delcine, sir."

"I hope so," was all the stranger replied. Delcine did not turn away out of respect for Mr. Casseus, but Jocelyn had the distinct impression that he would have under different circumstances.

Little changed in the weeks that followed as Mr. Casseus eased Mr. Delcine into his duties. Jocelyn continued to feel uneasy about the new manager, but did not allow his perceptions to cloud his judgment or impact his work. But much changed when Mr. Casseus handed the reigns over to Delcine.

At first it was small things. Delcine would just make snide remarks about how ugly Jocelyn was. Jocelyn was used to this growing up, and had been well trained by his mother to deal with it. "Well, I am as God made me," he might say, if Delcine demanded a response to his bullying.

Delcine found excuses to pay Jocelyn nothing for the types of jobs that Mr. Casseus had begun to pay him cash for. "This is part of your duties to live and be fed here," he would assert.

Then, Delcine would make fun of Jocelyn on his bicycle. "That thing is even more pathetic than you," he might say. Jocelyn would remain silent or reply, "Then we are well suited for each other," if Delcine pressed him.

Delcine called Jocelyn to the kitchen on numerous occasions to run errands to town. He would press money into the boy's hand, charge him with buying a cigar or some other small purchase, then spit dramatically on the floor. Pointing to his disgusting pool of saliva, he would say, "Return before that dries, or you will get a whipping." Jocelyn could not understand such mean-spirited behavior, but he jumped on his bicycle and made the best time he possibly could. The fact that sometimes he made it and sometimes he didn't, with all things being equal, led him to believe that Delcine may well have helped that saliva to disappear. For the beatings he *did* endure, he became masterful at selecting exactly the right branch (with which he was *also* tasked) so that it minimized his pain, yet avoided the risk of Delcine going to select a thicker one.

The last straw was the day when Delcine decided to mess with Jocelyn's cow. By this time, Jocelyn had had the daily responsibility for milking then moving the cows for several years. This was not a complicated task. It was not a task requiring great mental prowess. He had a wonderful system for moving the cows, always tying them responsibly, so that they had freshly grown grass each day, and they did not escape. Yet, one day, Delcine insisted on going early in the morning to milk. Jocelyn could not understand this.

When they arrived, his cow, and only his cow, was found dining extravagantly on sugar cane.

"Mon Dieu, Mon Dieu!" Jocelyn cried as he ran to her in a row of sugar.

"Stupid boy! Mr. Casseus will hear of this!" Delcine scolded. "You will get a beating when we return."

"Of course, Delcine. But…"

"No 'but,' boy!" Delcine yelled angrily. Jocelyn recognized madness in his countenance. He thought very hard about the previous afternoon when he had secured his own cow just as all the others. How odd a coincidence that it should be *his* that escaped.

Jocelyn endured his beating without the luxury of choosing his own branch that day. He also resolved that he would take extra care in securing her from that day forward. That afternoon he knew he was risking that this mother, expecting very soon, would not have access to enough grass to nourish her fetus, but he tied her rope very close, making many extra knots.

The following morning, when Jocelyn hurried to the fields to milk, he discovered that his cow was gone. He knew this to be *impossible,* considering how meticulously he tied the knots. Still, he milked the cows as expected and rushed back home for fear of further retribution.

After delivering the milk to the kitchen, and eating his morning meal, he was ambushed by Delcine as he began to return to the fields.

"How is your cow this morning? Fat from all her sugar?" Delcine asked acidly.

Jocelyn did not know how to admit to Delcine that his cow had again escaped his tether, so he said nothing. Unfortunately, saying nothing only angered Delcine worse.

"Your miserable cow escaped again, and now I have her in *jail*, boy, what do you say to that?"

"That's not possible, Delcine, she could not have escaped my knots," Jocelyn responded innocently. Desperately.

"Are you calling me a *liar,* boy?!" the man spat in Jocelyn's face.

Jocelyn thought to himself, 'that is *exactly* what you are,' but instead forced himself to form the words, "No, sir."

"Your cow can be returned to you when you pay me three dollars for the plants she ate, boy!" Delcine demanded with forced calm in his voice. "Do you understand?" Delcine knew well that he had cut off Jocelyn's access to cash, and this would be an impossible feat.

"Yes, sir," Jocelyn responded. He immediately grew desperate, also remembering that he had spent all his cash on buying this cow only a few weeks ago. Still, if he gave it a great deal of concentration, and prayed hard to God, maybe he would be delivered from this terrible situation.

That night, hoping that Delcine had not taken his anger out on the cow by starving her, Jocelyn prayed to God. He prayed and prayed that he could come up with three dollars to get his cow out of

Delcine's despicable jail. As he lay his head down to sleep, Jocelyn remembered that when he began earning money, he would hide it in different places. Perhaps if someone dishonest struck on *one* hiding place, he would go away happy with his findings. Jocelyn ran through all of the hiding places he could remember, and at last found FIVE dollars laying flat across the inside top of one of his prized shoes. Jocelyn rejoiced and made a plan to free his cow in the morning.

Jocelyn hurried to the fields to milk, assuming Delcine would not yet be up. He took extra care to fill the milk bucket as full as four years of experience told him he could reasonably carry back. That long walk gave him time to contemplate how miserable his life had become due to this horrible Delcine. He could do his job to the very best of his ability, but he saw no way that Delcine was going to change his view of Jocelyn.

He found Delcine taking his morning meal, went up to him respectfully and said, "Here is three dollars, Mr. Delcine. May I please have my cow back? I promise she will not go loose again" He reached his hand out, holding the bills. It nearly killed him, knowing that Delcine had been so obviously deceitful.

"Thief! Where did you get that money?!" Delcine demanded, throwing his food onto the ground. Jocelyn was shocked at this display.

"I *earned* it. Mr. Casseus paid me for my labor," he pled.

"LIAR! You spent all your money on that stupid COW!" Delcine insisted.

Jocelyn took several seconds to collect himself, but returned with great honesty, "I had thought so too, Mr. Delcine, but I prayed to God and he helped me remember that I had hidden money in my shoe." Jocelyn instantly regretted giving away that hiding place, but he was beyond worrying about his future with this wretched man in the interest of getting through this moment.

Delcine violently grabbed the three dollars from Jocelyn's hand, still outstretched, and threw it in the boy's face. Jocelyn didn't know if this was his invitation to bend down and pick up the money, or *what* he was expected to do. So he just stood there. Mute. Paralyzed.

"That's it, boy! Come on, fight me!" Delcine baited. He pushed Jocelyn's shoulder, nearly knocking him down. "FIGHT ME!"

* * *

Jocelyn opened his eyes. He saw Mr. Casseus standing between his position on the dusty ground and a bright sun.

"Come with me, boy," Mr. Casseus said with irritation. He walked away briskly, and Jocelyn recognized it was his duty to get up and follow, though his head was spinning. He noticed Delcine standing at a distance, glaring daggers, and holding his forehead above his eye.

"What's going on, Jocelyn?!" Mr. Casseus demanded.

"I *really* don't understand it, Mr. Casseus, sir. He doesn't like me..." Jocelyn felt he had nothing else to lose at this point. "He *lies*, sir. You *know* me. I have worked hard for you for four years. I am a good worker. I have changed *nothing*. He hates me!" Jocelyn lost his battle over his emotions and began to cry.

Mr. Casseus took inventory of the boy. He *had* been an excellent worker, but excellent workers were expendable. Managers with experience were not. With sadness in his voice, and a clear intention to rid himself of a problem as quickly as he could, Mr. Casseus muttered, "You're too much, Jocelyn. You have to go now." The finality in his voice told Jocelyn to collect his shoes, his cow, and go. Still overcome with tears, and now a fear of the sudden great unknown that lay ahead of him, that is exactly what young Jocelyn did.

* * *

You would think they would give me something. You would think they would give me couple dollars to put in my pocket. You would think they would give us a little bit something. They don't give me nothing. And when I left their house, and I pass by them very quietly, I said, 'Au revoir.' They don't answer me. They don't answer me. For so long, 12, 13 years old, I was over there working for him, all this time working me hard. That's why I have that problem right now, working so much.

XIII. Homecoming

If I did something wrong, I can see it. But one thing for sure, I know I wasn't, I can feel it, I wasn't a cup of tea. Because when I was growing up, I was very dirty. And when you're dirty, you don't have friends. Nobody wanna be next to you. And I really believe, I really truly believe I wasn't clean either, 'cause I don't have somebody talking to you. You know how somebody tell you, 'OK, hey, go fix your bed. You don't fix your bed right. Comb your hair. You don't comb your hair right. Take this shirt off. Put that shirt on. Put this pants on. Put this shoes on. Do this. Go brush your mouth. Go pray God. Go do this.' Nobody tell me this. After I left my mom house, even when I was over there with my mom, some of the stuff they tell, some of the stuff they don't tell you. Even we don't have a lot of things we can use anyway, because we don't have a toothbrush. We don't have soap. You know, sometimes, we can get a little bit of soap, but for a lot of us to share it. Never use lotion after shower. Never use it. I did nothing wrong, but maybe this why he was so bad to me. Now, when the guy who got angry with me come in, and I thought everything was gonna be all right. And for a good while, everything was all right. But for some reason, and I really believe too, now, I'm thinking this way. Maybe God send him so I can get a blessing. God send him to push me out of there, because something had to happen to get me out of there.

93

Jocelyn felt the world had come crashing down on him. The long walk back to his mother's house was enough time to pull his emotions together, but he was no closer to having a plan for his future than he had been the moment he said 'Au revoir' to Mr. Casseus. He still had his cow, at least, which he would make a gift of to Maman's new boyfriend, Da, in exchange for seeking refuge in their home until another job could be found. Though Papa Teti was still around, this shift in the household dynamic was the most significant change that had transpired in his long absence.

Amancia saw Jocelyn's drawn countenance when he appeared outside their home and ran to him.

"You are sick, Amos!" she assumed, which could be the only possible explanation for the light to have gone out in her joyous son's eyes.

"I was asked to leave," he confessed, his head bowed in embarrassment.

"Jocelyn Apo! WHAT did you DO?!" she demanded harshly.

It was almost too much that even his Maman could believe he had done wrong. "Nothing, Maman! I did *nothing* wrong! I swear to GOD!" His eyes remained firmly on his toes.

The gravity of his response convinced her. "Very well, I will go to Mr. Casseus tomorrow and get to the bottom of this!" Maman promised. She doted on her dearly missed son for the rest of the day, knowing that the simple food she could feed him would not compare with what he had been eating at the farm. It mattered little as Jocelyn had no appetite.

True to her word, Maman spent the entire next day, from sun-up until sun-down, walking to confer with Mr. Casseus. Jocelyn was not sure what to expect, but his disappointment felt complete when Maman came through the door and said simply, "Well, that's that."

In the course of the following days, Jocelyn had more and more difficulty walking. He realized that something had become wedged between his toes on the long walk, and despite freeing the apparent splinter of wood, his foot did not heal. On the contrary, it became badly infected, leaving Jocelyn bed ridden at length. At one point the foot worsened when some vermin began to make a meal of Jocelyn's poor diseased foot in the middle of the night! Weeks became months. Amancia ceased to recognize her once energetic, grateful son. He continued to pray every day. He did his best to eat and regain strength, but had wounds to care for beyond those of the flesh. Maman was the perfect nurse. Marinath would come around with her young baby, and this too cheered Jocelyn. But his good mood was impossible to maintain.

After several months of Jocelyn's being effectively bed-ridden, Maman decided she had had enough. "Amos, do you believe God is telling you that you are not meant to work? Has he left your foot sick to tell you that you have worked hard and now you should rest?"

For a moment, Jocelyn took his mother's words for face value – thought maybe God *was* telling him to enjoy a rest. But he *wasn't* enjoying the rest. Not at ALL. He desperately *wanted* to work! Amancia watched her son work this out in his head.

"No Maman!" he finally replied. "I want *so badly* to work, and God knows this!"

"Yes he does, Amos. Yes he does. So, you must have a little sickness in your foot for God to *remind* you just how joyous it is to work. And now you have discovered this. When the time is right, God will heal your foot and present you with the right opportunity he has in store, don't you think?"

"Yes, Maman, you're right, of course," Jocelyn mused. Why hadn't he considered this? He never questioned that this was part of God's plan, but maybe it was because God was saving a special, important job for him. He continued to pray for health and work, but gave it over to God to happen when the time was right.

Then the dream of the well returned, and with it, the sense of hope in the future it would always give him.

96

* * *

Jocelyn was walking again. At first he helped Maman grow a small garden, now that he had learned so much about cultivating God's land. The cow had birthed her calf, and Jocelyn helped Da care for the animals. The family was judicious about taking milk away from the calf; they might rob her of a few ounces of her mother's nourishment each day knowing they could get ten cents for it from neighbors. And once every couple weeks, Amancia encouraged Jocelyn to drink the milk to help him heal. This cow had been a good financial investment, and was now paying returns on his health as well as his purse.

Once the family was confident that Jocelyn's foot was only getting better, and he could spend most of the day working or standing on it, he would walk into town and look for work each day. "Hello, I am Jocelyn Apo," he would say to strangers, carrying himself tall and holding his shoulders as broad as he could manage. "I *love* to work, and, God bless me, I'm a fast learner. I can dig, farm, care for animals, build, clean, ride a bicycle, and do any kind of work you wish. I will work for very little. Whatever you can pay me. Please give me a chance to show you. God bless you." Jocelyn realized that some grown men responded very poorly to this approach – found it a bit pertinent even. But he believed that the *right* man would not be threatened by him, and *that* would be a good man to work for.

Woodensky was just such a man. "You're something else!"
Woodensky responded to Jocelyn one day soon after this job search had
begun. "I like you kid. I work at a fish farm. I believe my boss could be
convinced that we need help, especially if you don't ask for too much
money."

Jocelyn was thrilled. He had always loved fish, and he also knew
that working around fish meant water, which could be a blessing on hot
summer days. "God BLESS you, sir. God BLESS you!"

Woodensky taught Jocelyn how to hitch a ride through town on
the back of passing cars. On the back of an old red Citroen, Woodensky
prepared the boy by shouting terms and duties at Jocelyn over the
sputtering of a smoky engine. They arrived quickly at the fish farm of
Jean Vibert. Mr. Vibert, from the Bahamas, was the first white man
Jocelyn would work for. His property contained a large fresh water pond
where he bred fish to sell. He seemed a good man, a fair employer, and
Jocelyn thanked God for the new opportunity to learn about fish and still
live with Maman.

More than a year went by, and as promised, Jocelyn learned
quickly at Woodensky's side. The two would feed the fish, gather them
up in a net, and travel around Haiti selling the fish. The fish were
transported in a tank which they loaded onto a farm truck mostly empty to
prevent it from being too heavy, and one bucket at a time would fill with
water and finally live fish. This way, they could offer the freshest fish

possible at great distances from the farm. For short trips, Mr. Vibert entrusted Woodensky to drive and only the two employees would go. On longer journeys, he himself would drive. As the fish were sold, according to the wishes of customers, Woodensky and Jocelyn would get very busy with their knives gutting, fileting, and even removing the head or scales for fussier clientele.

Jocelyn earned 26 dollars every two weeks working for Mr. Vibert and was proud to be able to help Maman with her household expenses, and save quite a bit of money. He might have kept the job for longer except for one fateful day.

Late one evening, Woodensky and Jocelyn brought the farm truck back with the tank completely empty of fish. As they had been instructed, they took the time to empty the tank and offload it from the truck and placed it where it always resided, next to a small tool shed. Because of the late hour, they did not check in with Mr. Vibert, but each man went their separate ways home for a short sleep.

Early the following morning, Jocelyn arrived just behind Woodensky to the fish farm. Mr. Vibert was shouting at the faithful employee.

"What have you done with the tank, man?"

"Jocelyn and I emptied it late and put it where we always do – by the shed," Woodensky answered, confused at so odd a question. "We sold every single fish in it too."

"It is not there, you dirty liar!" Vibert returned angrily.

"I don't know what to say, Mr. Vibert, sir. That is exactly what we did."

"*I* think you STOLE it! Never brought it back here at all!" Vibert countered.

Woodensky became indignant at this accusation. "We most certainly did NOT!" Until Woodensky said, 'we', it hadn't even occurred to Jocelyn that he might be party to this accusation. Reflexively, the he began shaking his head vigorously to validate Woodensky's words.

Woodensky continued, "Please, take your truck, go to my home. You will see. There is NO tank there," he implored more reasonably now.

"No, there wouldn't be, would there, if you already sold it for even half of the *three hundred dollars* it cost me!" Vibert shouted. "You could hide that cash *anywhere!*"

Woodensky reached into his pockets and turned them out in a mocking gesture. This inflamed Vibert, who now flew at Woodensky. Jocelyn had never closed the distance between himself and his older co-worker, so was powerless to help when Vibert began punching at Woodensky's face. The employer took only a few well-aimed swings at Woodensky, who did surprisingly little to defend himself. Jocelyn

initially jolted forward in an instinct to come to his friend's aid, but caught himself in a *second* instinctive rush of self-preservation. He could not comprehend Vibert's reaction any more than he could the violent dislike Delcine had demonstrated toward him the prior year.

Jocelyn ran to a pile of clean cloths in the shed and dampened one. When he was confident that Vibert had finished with Woodensky and stormed off, Jocelyn gingerly approached his friend, writhing on the ground and bleeding profusely.

"Here Woodensky, my friend, here…" he whispered as he dabbed at the blood and tried to stop the bleeding that the man could not see for himself. "I'm sorry he did that… I don't know why he did that… I can't understand… Of course we just went home, did what we were supposed to do…" Jocelyn was talking as much to himself as Woodensky as he tried to nurse the man to a point he might be well enough to stand. Woodensky showed his gratitude with a simple pat on Jocelyn's knee as he let the boy care for him.

That was the end of any talk of the missing tank, and the mystery went unsolved. Woodensky and Jocelyn fed the fish and saw to other duties around the farm that day, and the following day a new tank was delivered to the farm. After about a week, Woodensky broke his silence on the matter and advised Jocelyn that he would find another job as soon as his face had healed. Although Jocelyn had always found Mr. Vibert a kind and fair employer until this, and appreciated the 26 dollars he earned every two weeks, he recognized that he did not want to be caught off guard again as he had with his heartbreak at the Casseus farm, so he, too, returned to his job search.

XIV. Father

*The next lady wasn't good either. They were a wealthy family
in Haiti. Their house is almost like a house here. A white house. They
got nice beautiful flowers. They got a black metal fence all the way
around, a nice beautiful fence. The gate to open is very tall, and then
at the end of it, they got something very sharp so nobody can climb on
other side. They got a long driveway. When you come to the
driveway, the driveway in the middle and their yard is on both sides.
The woman pay me, but when she cook food, she take all the food and
hold it in her living room where her family eat. After they eat, that's
when she bring some cold leftover food for me I can eat. One day, I
did ask her, 'Can you give me some food, please, before you take it
inside the house?' She said, 'No, we can't do that because when I sit at
the table with the family, we don't play around with the food.' And she
said, 'You will get more. When everybody finish eat, we'll bring the
food back to you guys.' That's what she did. For the maid who cooked
that food and for me, we only get it at the end. The maid can get in
trouble if the woman find out the maid gave me some of the food
before the family eat. They would put all the food in the plate or in
something. Put the whole thing, you know, put the meat in one dish.
Put the rice in something. Put the vegetable in something else. Put
whatever, sauce bean and whatever they have, put everything and
bring it inside the house. After you're done eat, and your whole family*

103

stop eating and you bring your food back to the kitchen so myself and the maid can eat.

Papa Teti also set out to find work for Jocelyn. In town, a wealthy family needed a young man to help around the house and work in the garden. Jocelyn made a good impression with his enthusiastic plea in person, so the Musac family granted him the live-in position. Of course, he would again be sleeping in an outdoor shed and expected to answer the calls of nature in similar fashion to his experience at the Casseus farm.

Jocelyn had seen government buildings at a great distance, and grand homes from an even greater distance, but the home of the Musac family was the grandest place he had ever been in person. He took great pride in caring for the many ornamental flowers in the front of the beautiful home, and the vegetable garden in the back. With no large farm, Jocelyn did not know how the Musacs came to have all the money that it must have cost to own this beautiful dwelling, but perhaps this is what it meant to truly be wealthy.

Inside the house, he was given occasional duties by the maid as well. There was a small room in the home which had a large pot that sat on the floor and held water that came out of the wall. With his bare hands, Jocelyn sat on the floor and scrubbed this bowl full of water, not quite sure of its function. One of the family's grown sons passed in the hallway and glanced in at him as he worked, but said nothing. Jocelyn might have taken a drink from the bowl of water, so foreign was this room to him. Later in his life, Jocelyn would reflect on this place and know that God was with him, preventing him from consuming toilet water.

When he rose and walked down a long hall to return outside, out of the corner of his eye, he saw another man walking soundlessly into a wall within a small guest bedroom on the main floor. This startled Jocelyn, so he backed up to check that the man was alright. Standing in the doorway, Jocelyn beheld his *own* image for the first time in his life in a medium-sized framed mirror that hung over dresser drawers. He had heard of mirrors, of course, and quickly guessed that this was what he saw before him. Jocelyn smiled. He scowled. He was unable to stifle a belly laugh at the sight of his scowl. He did not find himself as ugly as he expected to! Maman *had* worked hard to convince him whenever he was taunted. "I see you better than you see yourself, Amos," she would say. What a wonderful discovery to know she was not just trying to spare his feelings.

"Boy, what are you doing?" demanded the angry voice of the same grown son who had not bothered to offer Jocelyn so much as a rag to clean the toilet. "Come away from there!"

105

Jocelyn understood it was wrong and a terrible imposition to gaze into the family's mirror, but he would find, or *create* opportunities to do so repeatedly in the months he worked for the Musac family.

* * *

Running errands into town was a large part of Jocelyn's responsibilities to the Musacs. Over several months, he grew to know the many familiar faces of the shopkeepers, and even many of the customers themselves. Now that he had seen his own image, and had gained more knowledge of the world (and biology), the role of Hachacha Ojasma in his own existence became unmistakable. Still, Jocelyn avoided the man actively. He waited for God to guide him about the right thing to do.

Jocelyn continued his employment for the Musacs, feeling unsettled and certain that it was not part of God's plan for him. To his own shock, one day mid-morning when he saw the mistress of the house, he walked straight up to her and lied.

"I have a couple of cows, and the people who take care of them need me," he blurted. "There's a problem..."

Jocelyn wasn't quite sure what he was going to say if she interrogated him. Naturally he had no means of contact with the outside world, and certainly none that morning. Although he had *once* owned a cow he had long since entrusted to Da, so he knew he could at least embellish on cows if pressed, he truly mystified himself with this ridiculous excuse.

To Jocelyn's great relief, however, Mrs. Musac merely said, "Okay. Ça va!" and excused the young man.

Jocelyn grabbed his few personal effects and strolled down the road and through town. In the back of his mind he wondered what he would tell Maman about leaving a job for no real reason. But in the front of his mind, he was thinking of his father. The feeling that this inexplicable maneuver had something to do with finally coming face to face with Hachacha Ojasma grew and grew. He wandered into residential parts of town where he believed his father to be living. Turning a corner, he came face to face with none other than the man himself. Their eyes locked.

Jocelyn hesitated. He was initially speechless, then blurted, "You're my father," to the man.

A peculiar expression of joy and sadness washed over Hachacha's face. He said very simply, "I know."

Hachacha invited Jocelyn into his small home nearby. One of Jocelyn's sisters, Annamarie, whom he had met on the street some years before appeared to be visiting with her small child. The three adults sat on primitive chairs sipping coffee while the child played with stones on the dirt floor. Jocelyn came to learn how he had been watched from a distance, with great delight, his entire life. Hachacha had fathered three girls older than Jocelyn: Elianise, Annamarie, and Jocelyn (a girl with his very name) so when he, a boy, was born there was great celebration. There was no discussion of Hachacha's relationship to Amancia or his absence from Jocelyn's childhood, but Jocelyn gleaned that a great respect was paid to Papa Teti by all parties. He knew with certainty that going forward, *this* would be his family too. However, he did *not* know that becoming part of this family was about to change his life.

XV. Building

From that point, all this stuff was happening to me that way.
Seem like everything coming in a good way. Well, you know
something, at the time, my cousin Jacques was a very, very smart guy.
A very smart guy and an intelligent man. And he's always wanting to
do something. It's a lot of Haitian guys like that, too, in Haiti. They're
very smart. They don't have education. They never spent one minute
in school, but they're very intelligent. Very intelligent. He's the one
who come up with idea to build a boat. He did most of this work. He
can do almost anything. He got the power to do all this stuff. He was
a grown man. I think he probably be like maybe 30 or 35 maybe. The
rest, we basically was a young man. He want our help. It was a bunch
of young men and people also who knows what they were doing a
little bit better than us. We were there almost like a helper. We was
helping him. Helping him at one time. Not every day, but almost
every day we help. Almost every day after I get off from work from the
place, like on the weekend. In Haiti, a lot of time, people don't do
nothing on Sunday. A lot of time, unless it's the hospital or stuff like
that. And on Saturday, that's when a lot of people get paid. A lot of
them will work a half day. And then, anytime I get a chance, we go on
the boat. Or we go someplace else, work, make a little bit extra
money.

"You see, Jocelyn, Jimmy Carter is the president of the United States. That means something different in that country," Jacques spoke quietly, almost under his breath. The two stood in Hachacha's home, having just been introduced. Jacques looked over both his shoulders and continued. "The good people of that country, they know that we are poor here in Haiti. They try to send money. The Duvaliers," (he looked over his shoulders again) "have been a disgrace to the name 'president'," Jacques continued with measure yet passion. "I am building a boat to sail to the United States. With a leader like President Carter, I believe it would be a fine place to live. And you are very welcome to help out and join us."

Jocelyn thought often of his dream for the future to live in a *pays étranger*. This United States sounded like a wonderful place to him. But this was not like farming. This was not like learning fish. This was an entire world – completely new, fascinating, mysterious, and wholly unknown to him. He felt like he had spent a lifetime holding onto his mother's skirt, going wherever she went. Being separated from her by half a day's walk would be nothing to carrying out his dream. But was his dream God's plan for him?

Jacques noted Jocelyn's hesitation and offered, "Look, Jocelyn, come and help. Help us build a boat and tell no one. *Then* you decide what to do. It will take many months to build it. You will have all the time you need."

Jocelyn liked the idea of being of help to his newfound family, and of taking time to think about a different future. He was proud to have earned it, and would not betray Jacques's trust, not even to Maman. And, he would be learning another craft. One he couldn't be honest about, maybe, but a craft nonetheless. Attaching himself to Jacques, a man who knew more about the world than he, would set in motion one of the keys to his future. By now Jocelyn understood that God sent him angels on earth to help guide him. He would forever make it his job to recognize them.

Two weeks later, Jocelyn, Jacques, and two other cousins about his age whom Jacques had recruited met early on a Sunday morning to fell trees. Even they, once covering the island, were diminishing in number owing to the furniture industry taking but not replanting God's resources. The very remote area that Jacques had chosen to build was no exception; while there were no *people* around for miles, there were only the occasional mature trees here and there to choose from.

Out of the back of his truck, Jacques pulled two enormous store-bought saws with polished wood handles on each end and menacingly sharp teeth between. Pairing up, the men brought down ten trees that day. Jacques demonstrated to them how to lay down two logs as a base and cut the third tree into planks, which is what would be needed to build a boat. There was just enough time before sundown to cut one of the ten trees into seven planks: two rounded and five fine flat ones from the core.

"I will come every Sunday. *Every* Sunday," Jacques insisted. "Soon, enough men will be helping that we will have more men than tools! Check with me during the week, and I will tell you if you are needed, and for what job. This is a community effort," he continued. "If you have money to buy nails, glue, varnish, or tools, check with me. Many of us will buy our way onto the boat with our labors, and some will with money," he held up the saws. "Gedulien cannot build since his leg is lame, but he has given money to get us started. That's just an example. But as God is my witness, I will be sure that each man and woman seeking a place on the boat contributes in a fair way."

Jocelyn had not given that much thought to fairness in this project – in fact fairness was a concept he tried to spend as little time contemplating as possible, believing that GOD would see to 'fairness' in the full course of his life. Still, he admired that Jacques's plan was so thought out, and centered on consideration to *everyone*, and not just those who could pay money. At last, Jocelyn's hard work would carry the same weight as gold!

Before all light was lost, the four pushed their logs and planks behind a row of bushes, and etched mental notes of where they stood, on a green hill, between two prominent mountains. "Never, EVER leave tools, or anything that someone could link to *you* or ANY of our brothers working on the boat!" Jacques emphasized. "You need to understand, if our boat is found, it is merely our labors that are lost. If we are *discovered*?" he hissed, "We go to JAIL!"

Jocelyn and his young cousins had not doubt of the veracity of Jacques's claims. Jacques knew so much more of the world, and each of them was pleased to learn from what he shared.

* * *

Eighteen months passed. Eighteen months while Jocelyn worked at odd jobs at the sugarcane company and other smaller farms around town. Whenever he had the opportunity, whether evenings or weekends, he visited the boat with a friend or two. Jocelyn grew more confident every day in his decision to leave his homeland, but it was confirmed absolutely when his dream of the well returned to him once again. He made small, discreet trips to the dry goods store for glue, screws, sand paper. He agonized over the eyes on him, confident that they didn't have any reason to suspect him of wrongdoing, but lived in perpetual fear of what would happen if they did.

And, in the spirit of fear, Jocelyn worked long and hard to build the courage to tell his mother what he feared would break her heart, and he *knew* would break his own.

"Maman, you know my dream to go to a *pays étranger*?" he left off, hoping she would acknowledge him. But Maman, standing as she so often did over her boiling pot of laundry, did not even flinch. He continued, facing away from her and nervously chewing a piece of sugar cane. "My cousin, Jacques Ojasma… Maman, I am helping build a boat and I am going soon to the United States!" he finished hopefully. Only his concern for *her* held him back now.

"What if you don't make it, Amos?" she asked very simply.

"But what if I *do*, Maman? What if God makes sure that I *do*? I could take care of you. I could take care of Marinath. I could take care of Papa. I could take care of *myself*, Maman!" he pleaded with passion, still afraid to look at her.

She continued to stir, showing no emotion. "You've never been anywhere," she reasoned.

"I know, Maman. I know. But you have taught me well. God will guide me. I learn fast. I learn SO fast, Maman. You show me 'abc's one time. ONE time, and I get it. I will be smart and I will be careful, and I will work so hard…" He was painfully eager for her approval, but it broke his heart to leave her. Only the thought of doing well for himself in the United States and being able to make her life better every day so she didn't have to work so hard propelled him forward. She seemed to understand this.

114

"Just keep God in your life, *every* day, Amos. You do this, and there will never be a wrong decision." He caught her vintage maternal glare when he finally summoned the courage to face her.

Jocelyn thought his heart would explode. Somehow, knowing that she now knew of his plan did not bring the relief he thought it would. But he hugged her on his way out, and thought to himself that her embrace was one of the many memories he would have to wrap neatly and protect against whatever he would soon be facing.

* * *

After the planks were all shorn out, Jacques and the many men used water to bend and shape them, and ties and time as their accomplices. Next came much hammering. Great, large nails were driven with such tremendous manpower that many a man went home with left hands which did them no good for weeks following poor aim. The nails were sunk well into the wood, and copious amounts of glue filled the spaces behind them. Expense was not spared on this material either, and fingers were just as likely to be glued together for days as struck by a powerful hammer. If mishap during construction were to be any measure of the seaworthiness of this boat, Jacques and his team could be in no doubt of her strength.

As the vessel, twelve feet wide by twelve feet long, began to take shape, Jocelyn and many others could not fully comprehend how this over-sized canoe would hold the sixty-some people that Jacques had recruited as passengers. Of course, Jocelyn had spent no time on the open ocean and there was much about the journey that he could not yet comprehend. Two tall, removable poles with foot holds and two enormous sails were added at the end of construction. Jacques impressed upon the team that sea water would be their delivery, yet their enemy. The salt in the water would eat a ship alive if not properly prepared, and so again, expense was not spared as the application of many coats of salt-resistant varnish, both inside and out, were applied. Patience was demanded as the coats dried slowly in the humid summer days. But at last, in September of 1980, as Jocelyn approached his 19th birthday, the boat and its passengers were ready to set sail.

XVI. Goodbye

If they catch us, everybody would get beating and thrown into jail. Nobody is allowed to leave this country or to come to this country. United States have a policy for everybody. But in Haiti, people in Haiti, they take it away. All over, they take it away. You're taking a high risk in Haiti to escape Haiti and come here. If the government in Haiti catches you, you're in big trouble. I started to focus more into the boat, focus more into the boat and nothing else. No more job. No more looking for a job now the boat just needed little touching. But one day, I went to the people where I was living in the farm working for them. I was living at their house. I went there to ask them to borrow some money, to borrow like $3. I know that they have it, but they told me they didn't have it at that time. Because at that time, that's what I was looking for so I can buy some more equipment for the boat. But once he said no, I didn't tell him I'm looking for anything else. We are more focused, everybody put more energy until we finish the boat. No more work after that. Our plan is to get up early and to put the boat close to the water and escape Haiti.

When we take off, when I left my mother's house to go in a city, I'm going to stay in the city at my sister's house like for a week. I was so hungry. I was so hungry. My face almost looking like dirt. You can see it. You can count my ribs. So I was walking from my older sister's house to another family's house. And I'm walking over here, over there, I hope I see someone I know. I been doing this

117

constantly. All day. All day I been doing this. Everything all day for couple weeks. Finally one day I saw somebody I know, and I went to him like that, I say, hello, bonjour. I say to him, 'I'm not too good, do you have – can I have some money? You have money on you?' He reach in his pocket and give me three dollars! I say "Thank you, Jesus!" When he give me that three dollars, I said "Mister, Merci beaucoup!" If I take it right now it like three thousand. When he give me that three dollars it was an angel come from the sky. I turn around, I get some sandwich, I get the bread, I went to buy bread with the meat in it. I eat it up so fast and I feel good.

Jocelyn knew that Maman would not come into the city, there would be no farewell. He needed to be ready at a moment's notice, and right at hand for Jacques in the final preparations for the journey. On the morning he left to stay with his sister, Elianise, before they departed together, Marinath came to their childhood home with her now-three-year-old daughter, Edelime. The child expressed the emotions that the women withheld.

"Why you go away, Jocelyn?" little Edelime asked with sadness in her eyes.

"Who said I am going away?" he asked tenderly, but looked up at Marinath as though to reprimand her for telling the child.

"Maman says you go away soon," the child persisted.

"Oh, well, grown ups, they are always coming and going to work, right?" Jocelyn reasoned. "You will work one day too, Edelime. Right now your work is to take good care of your Maman and Grand-Maman, okay?" he knelt to her level. She only stared at her dusty feet. Recalling the day he left for the Casseus farm, and Marinath's sadness, Jocelyn flipped onto his head right in front of Edelime. The child squealed with delight. Marinath remembered that day well too, and, on cue, walked over to her brother and pushed him over by his gangly legs. Maman laughed, despite the great emptiness growing inside her.

Jocelyn brushed himself off with more vigor than was probably required for cleanliness, as though somewhere deep inside himself he hoped to brush away the bits of unpleasantness this day brought. In silence, he strode over to Marinath and squeezed her tightly. Quickly. But Maman – he held her for an eternity. He painfully discovered that his silence could not force stoicism that would never be a part of him. He began to openly sob as he held the person he loved most in the world. She had grown a little plumper, he thought to himself, thanks very much to his ability to help feed her these past three years. At last, he found the will to pull himself away from his equally tearful Maman with the idea of making her fatter still.

119

"I will always be your son, Maman. I will *always* take care of you. *Je t'aime de tout mon Coeur*," Jocelyn cried as he picked up a small package of the few belongings that would follow him to a new life.

"Take care, my Amos! Be very, very careful. I love you too!" Tears streamed down her face and neck faster than she could wipe them away. She crossed herself and prayed aloud, "Please heavenly father, I beg you watch over this beautiful soul, the one son you have let me keep. I have taught him well in your love and I pray, strike me down but please let my son reach safety and find the good life he has worked so hard for, Amen."

Jocelyn walked backward away from the house, lacking the strength to take his eyes away from the source of all his earthly security. At last he, too, crossed himself to echo his mother's prayer for him, turned, and silently sent up an equally urgent a plea for his family to be kept well.

* * *

The moving crew spent a week of nights getting the boat to the water. Jacques had found various hiding places half a mile apart between the building site and a safe place to put the boat in the water. Twelve strong young men, including Jocelyn, met at ten p.m. and shared in the task of carrying the boat to the next designated location. Most nights this took an hour or more. At last they put the boat in the water along a remote shore where they could do so without being observed, but Jacques feared they would not clear the island if they attempted their final launch there.

"It troubles me to say, we must launch from across the River Mapou, or we will never break away from Haiti," Jacques shared with his passengers in small numbers. "On Saturday night, our movement through town a few at a time will not draw attention. As soon as it is dark, I will sail the boat out along the outer shore, and you will find me there with the boat stocked of all we can bring. Follow my instructions *precisely* for your own safety and for the safety of one another. And, God willing, we will set sail in the early morning hours of His day."

Jocelyn committed exact directions to memory, and went over and over with Elianise to be sure they both understood them and remembered them the same. He was regressed to the mental fogginess of childhood as the concentration of all his financial resources over the summer had been on the boat, and he was growing weak and confused with hunger. As he wandered town during the days, in search of *any* acquaintance he might politely beg for any money for food, he thought over and over about Saturday night's plan. His prayers were answered when an old friend with whom he had taken First Communion placed three dollars in his hand. Jocelyn made himself the biggest sandwich of his life and wolfed it down, barely chewing.

Saturday evening came at last. Every decision was calculated. Jocelyn and all the passengers dressed in black, or carried outer layers to put over lighter clothing. He was advised that it would draw less attention to walk with other young men his own age. Traveling in groups of no more than three, the passengers, over the course of an hour, made their way onto the thin strip of land separated from the rest of the island by the river. To complicate matters, the police station stood at the very corner by which they all must pass, immediately adjacent to a sidewalk and wooden railing overlooking the river. And the police were known to be sitting outdoors on a nice evening, enjoying their view.

Jacques had orchestrated every step. Groups were advised to come from different directions. Don't be loud, don't be silent. Don't rush. Be casual. You would not have guessed that twenty people in Jocelyn's group hid trembling behind shrubs three blocks from the center of town when they took their turns strolling out at ten minute intervals. At last it was Jocelyn's turn. He and two of the young men he had worked with so many times sawing, hammering, and painting, walked through the town, their hearts beating hard in their strong chests. They approached the police station. Jocelyn screwed up his courage.

"Did I ever tell you about living on that farm?" he said casually to his co-conspirators.

"No," one managed nervously.

"Oh yes," Jocelyn continued. They were right alongside the police station on the railing side of the street. He stopped, leaned against the wooden crossbeams, and pointed into the sky. He spoke at a level he believed the police would just be able to make out what he said.

"I had to wake by the North Star. The North Star kept me from losing my job. Cloudy nights, though, they were the worst because I didn't know when to wake and I was so afraid to go outside to go pee pee that I wet the bed!" Jocelyn heard a snicker from the direction of the police station. For good measure, he turned to face the water, bent at the waist and leaned his elbows on the wooden railing, overlooking the river. The two friends followed his lead and quietly under his breath he said, "Let's count to fifty, then we go." They were the longest fifty seconds of Jocelyn's life, but he was sure he had succeeded in demonstrating they were harmless.

At last, they continued a casual pace along the walkway, and Jocelyn spoke again as though continuing a conversation. "This bicycle, it had no tires. No tires at all, but I taught myself to ride anyway. So one day, the boss sees me riding and tells me 'okay, that's your bicycle now.'"

They were clear. They were past the police without drawing attention. Jocelyn couldn't keep up this chatter that defied his natural shyness, and fell silent in anticipation of the next part of the plan. When they had walked a quarter of a mile, they were to run as fast and as silently as they could. They kept to the side of the road, their eyes darting at all times to hiding places they could take up if they should see headlights coming from either direction. During their sprint, a car *did* approach from the direction in which they were headed. They dropped to the ground in high grass, and the car passed without event. At the end of their sprint of three quarters of a mile, they knew they were in range of where the boat would be, so they walked again, and pricked up their ears to listen for one short whistle. They walked slowly. Almost soundlessly. They heard insects, wind in the trees, and beneath these, deafening silence.

Finally, a low whistle came from about 20 yards in front of them, to the right, on the shore. Through silent gestures, the three agreed instantly on the direction of the whistle, and headed through the treeline for the shore. There they paused, and waited several moments to hear the whistle again. When it came, they broke out through the trees. Less than a moment later, they were in a clearing, facing their magnificent boat under a starry sky, which reflected majestically on the endless ocean water spread out, black as ink, in every direction. Jacques stood on land with his hand resting on the boat's side where a rope ladder allowed entrance to the 30 passengers already aboard. Jocelyn and his friends climbed in and received direction, once again through entirely silent gestures, to seat themselves according to a predetermined arrangement. Making 'V's with their legs, the youngest and strongest men sat all around the sides of the boat. They would need to have access to the boat's edge to help with the sails or other labor. In the crux of their 'V', the next row of passengers would sit similarly, accommodating another passenger until the low, center groove was reached. The most fragile of passengers made a row perpendicular to the rest of these along that very groove. They alone would have the luxury of facing the direction of travel.

As the latest arrivals settled themselves, a cool, welcome breeze blew across the boat. Jocelyn felt it was God there with them to deliver them safely to a better life. He looked around the boat. The other passengers were waiting to gain his attention. They pointed to their ears for him to listen, then pointed in the direction down the road. Jacques shifted his watchful eye toward the treeline and back to the boat. There was apparently a system in place. After several moments, one man raised his hand. A few seconds later, a woman. Then two more people. With that, Jacques faced the tree line and let out a low whistle just like the one that had beckoned Jocelyn and his companions. Seconds later, a married couple emerged from the trees. When they climbed into the boat, the couple took up residence right in front of Jocelyn. He actually became excited with this game, eager to play, and eager to see his sister emerge from the trees.

So it went on for a half an hour more. Jocelyn's young hearing was acute, and he was quick to shoot up his hand whenever he detected sounds of human approach. Every few minutes, another small group joined them. He didn't have to wait long as Elianise came through the trees with another young woman within ten minutes of him. He did all he could to harness his enthusiasm, but knew his broad smile would silently convey all. His white teeth glowed in the dark night; his sister spotted Jocelyn immediately and was positioned across the boat where she could be reassured by her little brother's smiling face throughout the journey.

Jacques kept exact count, and quickly the sixty-one friends, relatives, and neighbors were accounted for. Bodies were packed tightly in the small space of the boat, and it was impossible for the travelers to ignore the energy radiating from one another. One might think that the great relief to have arrived to this point unscathed would translate to a collective sigh; an exhausted peace might come to rest on the shoulders of all. But instead, excitement gripped each and every one of them. A sense that this was not the end of an arduous challenge; rather, the beginning of an adventure. Jocelyn heard Maman say, "*Croiser les bras*," and, despite close proximity to the stranger in front of him, that is exactly what Jocelyn did.

Jacques picked up a long pole, carved from one of the rounded-edged planks left over from the great trees used to build the boat. He climbed the rope ladder and laid it inside the boat as he took up his position, compass in hand, at the leading tip of the boat. He instructed two young men to untie the sails as he wedged his pole at an optimal angle against the shore and, with raw adrenaline, pushed sixty-two souls out to sea.

Gold from the Well
Jocelyn Apo

XVI.   October 5

There's a lot to talk about right there in that moment because the boat was really nice. It was painted really good. It was strong and everything. Nobody felt scared. We had a sail and we had this thing in the back of it like you're driving a car. A rudder. But we don't have a motor. We have a sail to catch the wind. During the day, we don't have wind. There with was no wind during the day, but every night we got wind.

When you sit in one spot, the only time you want to move is if you want to come to the edge of the boat and you want to do number two. Whether it's men or women, you're going to do number two in front of everyone. It's no big deal. Nobody pays attention anyway. That's how it was. We were very tight. Somebody was between my legs and somebody always sits between every person's legs. I would have myself and four or five people sit in a line like that, between each person's legs.

As the boat began to drift, the sails unraveled and instantly grabbed the breeze God sent them. Jacques moved swiftly to direct the sails then take up a firm grasp of the rudder and point them straight out to sea. Jocelyn and many other young men on the outer rows of the boat raised their heads into the wind to feel the crisp air blow over their smiling faces. No one dared make a sound, but

129

singing rang so loud in Jocelyn's head he felt sure others could hear it.

Very soon, the homeland was a mere dot on the horizon, and splashing of the waves all around them was the only sound that could be heard. The movement of the boat ranged from gentle rocking to violent jolts. For most, including Jocelyn and his sister, this was their first time off land. The initial excitement that had been palpable morphed temporarily into a quiet, almost cozy peace. But as they continued their fast pace over choppy waters, inevitable sea sickness gripped many. This would be the first of many realizations of just how challenging basic human functions would be in these tight quarters.

First, it was actually Jocelyn's sister, Elianise who became ill. He was powerless to come to her aid as he watched her, from across the boat, clutch at her stomach, then move her hands to her mouth in a futile effort to retain the last full meal she would know for many, many days. It had been the strategy of most aboard to indulge as best their purses would allow, but now it was all for nothing. Perhaps only a dozen actually vomited, at their various positions in the boat, but that was enough for the first of many wretched odors to encapsulate the passengers. A few, including Jocelyn came to the aid of others, using the shirt off his back to clean the sick, drag it through the waters as best he could reach without capsizing them, and use it again, wet, to finish the job. This practice would prove to be standard routine within a few hours as physical demands grew.

Residual excitement, adjustment to the motion, and most of all the tight proximity of others kept everyone wide awake as the sun began to emerge at their backs. They sleeplessly welcomed its warm rays, though regaining a view of their horizon brought into sharp focus just how isolated and vulnerable they truly were. Confident, now, of their safe distance from land, Jocelyn began to hum a gospel tune learned for his First Communion, and was soon joined by many others around him. As the morning grew warmer, the wind slowed and the rocking waves steadied. A few people even dozed off at modest intervals.

The younger, more agile passengers, most inclined to be at the outer edges of the boat, sat strategically to relieve themselves over the side. As Jocelyn was among the lucky ones to keep his last meal down, he was also among the first to try squatting over the side. Only an upbringing which made little fuss over such an act could have allowed 62 people, many strangers to one another, the relative comfort in adapting to this act. But the seas were not as forgiving as the company.

"It starts to come but the water pushes it back!" he lamented quietly to Jacques. His older cousin let out a belly laugh and said simply, "Well, then, remind it who is the boss!"

The passengers stuck in the center of the boat could not readily get to the side, and there were those whose fear of drowning (many did not even know how to swim) demanded a method not unlike the removal of vomit from the bowels of the boat. Rows of people unceremoniously passed soiled articles of clothing to the braver young men at the outer edges to be cleansed in the more placid waters. As only so much could be accomplished in this way, human refuse became the second odor to slowly take the passengers prisoner, and wearing at least *these* articles grew more optional by the day.

There was an unspoken understanding that rations needed to be stretched. Jacques could only guess at the duration of their trip, and though space did not allow for a month's worth of food and water, he feared that in a worst case scenario they could be adrift that long. There was always a chance that they would run aground elsewhere, and this notion was at least as terrifying as running out of supplies if it were the wrong government whose hands they fell into. Still, enough of these people had been close to starvation and deadly thirst to know they were better off consuming what they had and hedging their bets for the future. So, after many hours in the sun, Jacques brought out a bottle of water and it was dispensed in equal capfuls to everyone until the bottle was gone. Likewise, a handful of ripe mangoes were cut and shared, understanding that spoiled fruit in three days would do them less good than good fruit today.

As the sun set that day, the wind picked up. Any who had managed to doze a little during the calm daytime drifting were jolted back awake. Jocelyn was not among them, and would, in fact, be awake for days to come. Seasickness returned to a few, though with so little in their stomachs, dry heaving was much more prevalent than actual vomiting. But after a successful day, and the promise of another clear night by which Jacques could navigate by the stars, he set the sails and rudder confidently, then broke the relative quiet by addressing the entire boat.

"This was a good day. We make a good team. Not every day will be as full of promise as these 24 hours have been, but God willing, I believe we will make it to Miami quickly."

A measured cheer went up among the passengers, all of whom were prepared to cling to any bit of reassurance. Jocelyn crossed himself and thought of Maman, as he had many times throughout the day, and began to hum his tune again. In a ripple, many around him likewise crossed themselves, and as darkness settled, whether sleep came for all or not, a sense of community carried them all through another night of rough waters

Gold from the Well
Jocelyn Apo

.

XVII.   October 6

Everybody was cooperating very good. A lot of time we do try to get a little sleep in the boat. We do try to get a little sleep, but because we rock back and forth so bad, you can't focus to sleep like that. If you in the middle, you can sleep better, so we take turns in the middle. Another thing too, once in a while you get wet. When you try to doze off a little bit, the waves come and just cover everybody and everybody has to scoop the water out of the boat because you cannot keep the water in the boat because it'll make it too heavy. We don't want to sink. Way over here we saw ships going far out. If we try to do something, they won't stop. We was in too bad condition.

Another sun rose at their backs. Another rough night was replaced with a calm morning. Seasickness was slowly replaced with thirst and hunger, but not to a degree that was novel for any of the passengers. Jocelyn greeted the day in his usual manner, thanking God for another sunrise, even if he wouldn't eat.

All excitement had worn off, but most aboard were yet to be terribly stressed physically. Among the many days adrift, the early days beyond the first would prove to be the easiest. Sometime after noon, Jacques' right hand, a burly man of perhaps 25 by the name of Makenly, climbed the larger of the two sail poles to report if anything could be seen on the horizon. When he gazed behind them to the east, he shouted.

"Hey! There is a boat. A ship, I think. Come and see, Jacques!" Makenly scrambled down the pole to make way for Jacques to ascend.

Jacques made his way gingerly from the back of the boat where he had manned the rudder somewhat futilely as there was almost no wind. Apologizing as he stepped on body parts, he shot up the pole the moment Makenly came down. He strained his eyes. With the sun now crested and beginning its journey down the western sky, Jacques had a clear view of the ship, some five miles away. Jocelyn craned his neck to see the ship, but was unable from his level.

"That is one big ship!" Jacques marveled. The passengers watched as his gaze moved slowly from the north to the south. "Probably a luxury liner," he began to climb down with less energy than he had exerted going up. Most of the people in the boat watched him with anticipation for further explanation, so he continued.

"Probably Americans. It is a ship that they take a holiday on. It has bedrooms and kitchens and they visit islands in the Caribbean."

Jocelyn contemplated the irony of this. His imagination about his *pays étranger* was often very vivid, but one thing he could *not* imagine is ever wanting to travel back over these waters on *holiday*. Many others must have been thinking the same thing, because there arose a small murmur as people spoke softly amongst themselves.

"Something to eat?" Jacques suggested softly as he made his way back to the rudder where the supplies were tucked neatly away. He pulled out two chunks of bread and gave them to those nearest him to be passed around. Each man and woman took little more than a Communion portion. In fact, most placed their morsel in their mouths and savored them there like a sacramental host, in part because they were conserving water and the bread brought forth saliva, sparing them the sensation of thirst. So accustomed to hunger were these people that there were no longing eyes fixed on the bread chunks as they grew smaller and smaller on their respective paths around the boat. None whatsoever. Rather, each man and woman aboard knew that a day with something small to eat was a good day.

This small bit of nourishment served as entertainment for an hour or so, and after a hot afternoon, the wind began to pick up with ominous strength well before sunset. Jacques again ascended the pole and looked to the south, the direction of their wind.

"I see clouds. I think maybe a storm is coming," he observed with hesitation in his voice. There was a collective sense of fear, but he continued. "Don't forget what we have discussed. This boat is sound. Built to stand up to water, inside and out. But just remember if the waves come over the sides, we must remove water as quickly as we can." Many nodded in understanding.

As the waves grew more and more violent through the early evening, methods were put in place to remove the water which quickly found its way to the bottom ridge of the boat. The empty water bottle and a few straw bowls and vessels that had found their way aboard made circular trips to the center and back out again where young men, including Jocelyn, held onto them dearly (though soaked through) and emptied them swiftly.

With no visibility of the stars above, Jocelyn guessed, based on the length of time it had been dark, that it was around midnight when the skies opened up on them.

It rained a couple of times, but nothing too bad. We were very lucky for that. We were crazy because that was a warm month. The only thing we had was a little wave here and there, that's it. I couldn't believe it. But we learned we could go day after day without water or food more than people may think. I'm sure the people who study it, they probably have an idea how many days people can go without water or food, we could be in that. A lot of them probably see that too, when Haiti had the earthquake, that a lot of people last for a very long time with no food or water.

When the rain came down, first in a strong downpour but soon diminishing to a trickle, everyone instinctively lay their heads back and opened their mouths. But the waters remained extremely rough, so now that all the passengers were bouncing around with their heads back, vertigo quickly ensued. Nobody had truly been expecting an end to their thirst, and the fresh water was welcome in whatever quantities they could capture. Keeping it down was another matter altogether.

The early morning hours passed with little variation, so when a cloudy sunrise delivered them from such violent waves, the frustration of minimal daytime movement that the prior two days had begun to foster was forgotten. Many of the passengers made the clear discovery that, blinding rays or no, daylight hours would be their best opportunity to try to sleep. Jocelyn still had not even really attempted to, and he had the extreme disorientation to prove it.

By midmorning the clouds had burned off, and been replaced by intense humidity they all knew well, coupled with a very hot sun. By early afternoon even the humidity broke, and the skin of every passenger began to feel like pulled leather from the salt water washing over them all throughout the night, and the rapid drying as the sun beat down. There was no shade to retreat to. The water that remained was held for emergency. There was not even the room to stretch oneself out for adequate airing or rest.

A middle aged woman near the bottom of the boat began to moan seemingly involuntarily. Another woman nearby leaned close to her, and after the two exchanged whispers through parched lips, the neighbor announced softly, "She is not well. She needs our help." With that, the sufferer's eyes closed, and nobody was quite sure if she was resting or had passed out.

Jacques removed his shirt and passed it toward the women. "Shield her from the sun!" he directed. Several other men, including Jocelyn, quickly did the same. The long stick used to push them out to sea still lay in the bottom of the boat so, confident the smooth waves would do nothing to cause it to be lost, the articles were laid over it and its ends rested on the sides of the boat nearest the woman, threading precariously through the shoulders of those closest to the edges. By default a few others basked in the shade, yet nobody fought or argued for those prized positions.

The hot afternoon passed miserably for all the others, but when the sun began to descend the horizon ahead of them and they realized that, though the wind again picked up, the waves were almost as smooth as day, a general sense of relief took over.

Jocelyn leaned over to one of his young Ojasma cousins and whispered, "Hey, you know the one about my Maman and her three babies?"

"What? No. What are you talking about?" the cousin asked quizzically.

"The joke. The joke about Maman and her three babies!"

The cousin stared back at him blankly. "Well come on then, let's have it!" he returned, eager for a little bit of lightheartedness.

"Well," Jocelyn leaned very close. "My Maman, she had three babies. One went underground, one sat upon the ground, and one just went away."

The cousin contemplated this. "I give up" he said after straining his foggy brain.

Jocelyn went through a silent and restrained pantomime. "One went into the ground," (his rude gesture implied urination), "one sat upon the ground," (an equally rude gesture implied defecation), "and one just went away," he fanned at his backside to imply a gaseous emission.

141

The cousin shook his head and laughed, shoving Jocelyn for his juvenile joke. Jocelyn too was giddy with laughter and sleep deprivation. He held his sides in a happy discomfort.

As the sun set, Jocelyn leaned back against the side of the rocking boat and drifted pleasantly to sleep.

XIX.   October 8

Haiti and Cuba is the best friends in the whole world. There a
great relationship with Haiti and Cuba. And they see a lot of Haitian
boats coming by at Cuba. Some people that leave Haiti, they go into
the city and stay in Cuba. We plan to go to United States, though. No
Cuba. No Nassau. We want to go to United States.

Jocelyn slept in odd patches throughout the night. It was troubling how sheer exhaustion and extreme discomfort battled one another to be supreme ruler of his mind. At last when the bright rays of another scorching hot day came above the eastern horizon behind them, discomfort won out and Jocelyn was fully awake, as was most of the boat, though many like him seemed to have actually rested at night as God intended.

As passengers were gathering themselves, a few taking a turn at the edge of the boat for obvious reasons, the woman who had suffered so badly the prior day began to sob. It became abundantly clear to the rest of the boat that thirst and starvation had not succeeded in warding off her monthly visitor, and whether the embarrassment or the proverbial last straw, she was simply not equipped, in any sense, to manage this new problem. Everyone gave her the privacy she needed by way of their respectfully averted eyes and silence on the subject, so within a few moments she had regained her composure. The same neighboring young woman who came to her aid the day before soothed her and casually saw to a short term solution which reflected how scarcely *all* of their fundamental needs were being met. Almost nothing to eat. Almost nothing to drink. Almost no way to move. And no shelter from the water, the sun, the wind, the salt.

At what would be dinnertime, Jacques opened a bottle of coca-cola and, using the cap from the empty water bottle, dispensed it in miniscule amounts equally to all. Like the bread two days before, most held their capful in their mouths as long as they could before joyfully swallowing it. There was no promise of rain for water, and he was holding the last bottle of water until the last possible moment, but when the wind picked up well before sunset, concerns for another very rough night of nausea and bailing seeped into the minds of everyone.

Sensing this despair, Makenly demanded the compass from Jacques and took the liberty of climbing the tallest pole for a last look before the sun set. After many minutes at the top of the pole, repeatedly consulting the compass, he angrily shouted down, "Hey, I think we are headed for Cuba!"

"No, I don't think we will hit Cuba," Jacques shouted back calmly. But Jocelyn noted how he scanned the boat for reaction to this claim.

"Yes we are!" Makenly insisted, now climbing down the pole. When he reached the bottom, he continued his accusations. "We

agreed! We are going to Miami. Not Cuba. Not Bahamas. MIAMI!
This boat is clearly going to stop at Cuba!"

"We are doing our best to navigate, Makenly," Jacques
responded, more forcefully now. "Yes, we will pass closer to some of
the islands than others. And we *may* pass near to Cuba. But Cuba is
a friend to Haiti, and we must take our chances to *stay on course*."
He finished so definitively that Makenly had no choice but to back
down. Makenly took up a standing position at the leading edge of the
boat, feeling the increasing wind on his face and eventually cooling
down. Meanwhile, after enjoying the small bit of entertainment in
another prolonged, tiring day, everyone aboard began to contemplate
the prospect of stopping in Cuba.

A very rough, sleepless night of soaking, dizziness, and
bailing only served to sweeten that prospect.

Gold from the Well
Jocelyn Apo

XX.   October 9

They very used to boats coming by from Haiti at that time.
Haiti known for its gold. So they bring stuff to trade for gold, clothes,
whatever, in Cuba. It never our plan to stay in Cuba. Yes. But
people need a break. We was already needing a break.

The clear morning sun through a cloudless sky brought the
promise of a calmer day, but it took a couple hours for God to make
good on that promise. By the time the sun had put some space
between itself and the eastern horizon, everyone aboard was
exhausted from what seemed like the most violent night at sea yet.
Many fell asleep when at last the waves settled, despite the fast
climbing temperature.

Midday, Jocelyn heard a murmur from the front of the boat.
He lifted himself as best he could without upsetting the delicate
balance, and saw land. The murmur grew into a great deal of
clamoring.

"It's Cuba," Jacques pierced through the noise. "Everyone at
the edge – tell me what you can see."

Jocelyn craned his neck even further. Suddenly a young man
closer to the front of the boat shouted, "There are very bright lights.
They are flashing bright lights out to sea at us. I think they see us."

Jacques again surveyed the passengers. All had known hardship in their lives. Every single one. Yet, he had trouble believing they weren't *all* very near the end of what they could endure. He caught the eye of the woman who had had the most trouble in the middle of the boat and knew what he must do.

"The lights are a beacon. They mean for us to stop. We will have a short break before we resume our trip to Miami. This is something we *all* need," he directed, making a special point of catching Makenly's eye. Now that land was actually in sight, Jocelyn could tell from Makenly's reaction that even *he* was eager to place his feet on soil again.

The slow motion of the boat meant that it was another half an hour before they reached land, but by that time three young teenaged boys, (the ones who, it turned out, had been flashing bright flashlights at them), were able to anticipate where the boat would come ashore and were waiting there. They rushed right into the water as soon as the boat was close enough and began to pull the vessel in. Jacques and Makenly jumped into the water to help, so Jocelyn and several other young men followed suit. The Cuban boys were less than subtle about lifting their shirts over their faces to endure the odor that washed ashore with 62 sea-weary Haitians.

Jacques laughed. "Oh, yes!" he said in Spanish, and was only understood by a handful of his boatmates. "We know too well how badly we smell!" With this, he gestured dramatically, waving his hand in front of his face so that his boatmates would understand what he had said. Many aboard nodded and were giddy to wash in the shallow, safe waters.

When the boat was far enough up on the sand that it would not drift away, the remaining passengers were helped off. Nobody moved naturally. Stiff muscles and shaky balance dominated everyone's slow crawl onto land. But after more broken Spanish from Jacques and some urgent gestures between the boys, Jacques announced that they would need to move the boat into the nearby jungle for security. Jocelyn and the other young men who had been part of the team who moved the boat to the water the prior week took up positions around the now much heavier boat for all the water it had absorbed. In combination with their respective weakened states, this was not an easy task, but finally they felt confident about the boat's position off the shoreline.

Jocelyn returned to the shoreline where he saw many of the passengers bathing themselves in the ocean. Many of the women had already finished with water and had made their way among the trees seeking out the leaves that could be employed to restore oils to their leathered skin. Jocelyn welcomed that thought, and the thought of bathing, but first he lay his body on the sand, stretched every muscle out as long as he could, and said a prayer to God for getting them this far safely.

Within an hour of their arrival, four men with backpacks came out of the jungle. It was immediately clear that they were associates of the boys, whose job it was to bring refugees ashore for purposes of trading. The men opened their backpacks and communicated with Jacques, once it was established that he was both the leader and the most capable of understanding what they said.

"I know we are all hungry," Jacques said. "These people have Carnation milk and bread to trade, so please, if you can, come and offer your belongings."

Jocelyn was blown away with how readily his boatmates relinquished what were surely precious items to have been brought along on the arduous journey. Immediately, several women walked to where the men were, reaching around their necks for prized necklaces. Men here and there reached into small sacks they carried to take out a nice shirt or gold bracelet. Jocelyn looked down at the new watch he wore; it no longer held the value for him that something to eat did. Soon the Cuban men were walking back into the trees.

Jacques lamented, "Sorry, but they did not have an opener for the milk, so we must do our best with rocks." He dispatched Jocelyn and two other young men to seek out strong jagged rocks from the shoreline, then pound at the steel cans strategically so as to puncture but not destroy the tops. At last a small hole was achieved in each, and five opened cans were passed around, and more were saved for later.

Cleaner, sheltered in the shade of tall trees, still, and now enjoying coin sized drops of milk in the palms of their hands, every one of the boat's passengers felt a great sense of relief. Long after the sweetened, condensed milk was gone, Jocelyn continued to lick his palm, as though the mere memory of the milk there were enough to satisfy him. Everyone in the group had grown so accustomed to a collective quiet in the interest of best preserving whatever nutrients or water were contained within their bodies that now, in the peaceful woods where wind through the leaves and birds overhead sung, they felt at total peace with one another.

* * *

After a long midday nap, during which most slept better than they had in weeks, many of the younger people, especially Jocelyn, felt the urge to move around. With a stern warning from Jacques not to become lost or come in contact with any other Cubans if it could be helped, Jocelyn set out with his sister in the late afternoon to walk at a leisurely pace to conserve their energy. He had known how bittersweet it could be to test the limits of his body with extreme work or travel, but Jocelyn was shocked at how strenuously his body objected to this old man's stroll through the jungle. They took great

151

care to remember their path and not stray for too long, in case the group had to leave emergently.

Jocelyn and Elianise searched high and low for any sort of food. He thought for sure he might recognize the tell-tale above ground foliage of yams, or surely a plantain tree, but none were to be found. Soon they thought it prudent to return to the camp, where the only thing they had missed was some spirited story telling.

At nightfall, every man and woman stretched themselves out and beheld a sky full of stars through openings in the canopy without becoming dizzy or ill. Though Jocelyn knew this was a temporary respite, he crossed himself and again thanked God for a break, and for making it this far safely.

XXI.   October 10

So we did stop in Cuba. We slept outside, not in the water. We slept outside. While we were in Cuba, I got to see where Cuba shot a US airplane in the body of water and on the rocks. I saw that. I saw where Castro shot down a US plane under JFK. It was a body of water, some type of water, no flight zone or something.

The group woke up at intervals to the calls of animated birds and the now unfamiliar sensation of filtered sunlight. Somehow the luxury of being dry on land gave many of the passengers a craving for coffee they hadn't dared even let into their conscious minds while bouncing on the waves the prior five mornings. In the absence of coffee, however, a few more cans of carnation milk were opened and passed around. It was thick and sweet and savored by all.

The Cuban boys who greeted the group had come and gone throughout the prior day. Late in the morning they reappeared, and asked Jacques in Spanish if anybody cared to see an American plane. When Jacques translated, Jocelyn jumped at the opportunity to see anything American. He was among a large group that was feeling restored and up for a small adventure.

The group broke out of the trees back onto the shoreline. Jocelyn marveled at the beauty of the Lord's beautiful ocean, which had nearly swallowed them whole the night before last. They walked a couple miles down the shore and the young boys pointed out to sea. Since nobody in attendance spoke Spanish, the boys gestured, simulating rifle shots. Stuck in a sandbar not far offshore, the tail of a military plane stuck out of the water, probably many years after it had gone down. The boys then gestured to some large boulders at the treeline, where the cockpit of the plane had landed. Jocelyn knew Cuba as a friend to Haiti, so he was filled with mixed feelings about his would-be *pays étranger.* But the longer he lived, the more he began to appreciate that situations could be complicated. Mr. Casseus had been in a difficult place between himself and Delcine. He himself had been in a difficult place between his father and Papa Teti. Maybe the United States was in a difficult place, and this pilot paid with his life. Jocelyn crossed himself again, saying a prayer for that pilot, and they headed back to the camp.

Before the boys left the group again that afternoon, they told Jacques that the group had to leave. In the morning, the grown men would be back again and would help tow their boat out beyond the sandbar which they and the American plane knew well, and return them on their journey. This was a bittersweet thought, but again the Haitians were of one mind, and that mind was set on Miami.

XXII.   October 11

The very next day, they came with a big boat and they helped
us out so we don't go in the wrong direction. Because some places in
Cuba, if you get in the middle of it, you're not coming out, that's the
water that they have set up for the enemies or something like that.
Once we left Cuba, they were such nice people, they pull us far
enough where they can. Now, you're talking about ocean water. This
is not a joke. The only thing you can see is the sky and water. Once in
a while, you can see one of those big ships very far away as he was
passing by. But even if they see you far, they have to go far from you
because they carry heavy waves with them also. If they come close to
us, we're going to be in trouble, they're going to turn us upside down.

Afloat again, out in the open ocean, the group was restored, yet
melancholy. Those aboard who had an education in geography had a
sense that if the trip to Cuba had taken four days, surely they had weeks
ahead of them. If this were so, they did not share these sentiments with
the group at large. Especially Jacques, who DID have just such an
education, and was painfully aware of what water could be collected, and
what bread remained to sustain 62 people for so indefinite a time.

After a mere 40 hours of shade, stretching, and relief, travel under
the hot sun all day wilted any spirits that had been refreshed in Cuba.

Jocelyn, a man who had worked a farm, actually thought of *himself* in this way. He knew that a wilted plant was not a dead plant. A wilted heart was not a dead heart. Never, once, did he believe he wouldn't make it to his *pays étranger*. He would just need a healthy dose of fresh, clean water when he did.

By now the group had come to associate the hottest days with the roughest nights, and this night presented no disappointment to the pattern. The jungles of Cuba would live on in their memories that night and for years to come as a virtual Garden of Eden in the midst of Hell.

XXIII.   October 12

Nobody can come out of the boat because the water too deep. The water very deep and you can't even see down below it. There's some places where we can see below it. We see a fish. We see this big thing running around from below it in the middle of the water, a lot of it, it doesn't move. It's almost like a river. Middle, a little bit middle of it. And a good portion of it is just like that. We saw sharks. We saw them jumping in the ocean and we saw them on the top, but we tried to stay away from them. We got scared. Because when they jumped, some of them did jump higher than the boat. It's just like when a wave comes, the wave is higher than the boat. That's why we get covered with water. Sometimes they go very fast and you see them running past you and they just go in a circle. But those guys on the boat make you feel good because they don't have a weapon, but they have something that if something was dangerous, they will try to fight with it or something. They've got something like a stick and they make a point, a point on a stick. Anybody in there, those guys would definitely do something. That shark may not have a chance. It didn't happen too often. It was just every once in a while. I guess probably in the water where they like to be or something. Remember, everything is wide open and that's where they live. When you're in the wrong spot, you're going to see them. You're going to see 20 fish or you're going to see one fish, because they're there. They are right in the water. You're

going to see them jumping and do all kinds of stuff. But the rest of it, I
tell you, it's so blue, too big, you can't feel nothing. It make a lot of
noise. A lot of noise, all day and all night.

XXIV.   October 13

When we have a wind, our boat was driving pretty good. It's almost like something with a motor in it. But when we didn't have wind, it doesn't go anywhere. We're going very, very slow. We're just moving very slow. You can walk as fast as the boat. It was tough. But sitting on the boat, you've got a lot of things on your mind. You know, when we're going to get there, and when you get there, is the United States going to return you Haiti? If they do return you to Haiti, when you get to Haiti, are you going to go to prison, are you going to go to jail, are they going to beat you up, no food, no nothing? You've got all kinds of stuff and it's true if the United States said no.

Gold from the Well
Jocelyn Apo

XXV.   October 14

Sometimes we singing. We do little bit shaking our body. We cannot move too much because otherwise, we don't want the boat to flip. But there was a time when we did a little bit singing. We sing of Jesus. We singing one song is about Jesus. Jesus is our brother. He's always looking over us. He will never let us peri. Peri is almost like destroy something. Peri means when you destroy something, you will never see it again. Never, ever, ever. That's what peri means. It means like you bury something, not even when somebody die because you may see 'em again. You bury something and you never gonna see it again. That's it. That's what peri is. And we say Jesus would never, never let you peri. Jesus is not gonna let anything bad happen to us. That's what we were singing. We call Jesus, Jezi. And then we'd pray. Yes, we prayed. We prayed for St. Mary. We pray for St. Mary to bless us, to keep us safe. We say, "Saint Mary plant the seeds, Amen." So we say that Mary is one lucky lady and God always be with her and we asked her to be with us today to bless us so we can make it to the dry land.

Yeah. We're singing this song that say I'm the spirit. All we say, we say, 'Lord, we're in your hands. You're our father and we believe in you.'

Gold from the Well
Jocelyn Apo

XXVI.   October 15

Desperation gripped every passenger aboard. Catching rain when they were lucky enough for it to fall was not enough to sustain them.

"Swallow. Swallow your saliva," Jocelyn would advise the people around him.

But eventually, there was no saliva to swallow.

When, on this day, the boat had reached a near standstill, Jocelyn leaned over the edge to gaze down at his reflection in the near glassy sea. The bottom was visible a mere ten feet below. He strained and reached down and cupped the water, bringing it to his face. At first he meant only to cool his hot skin under yet another scorching sun, but as he licked his lips, he noted that the water was not as salty as the water that hit them violently at night. He took another handful and sipped it. It was deliciously refreshing. It wasn't like well water, but at least it wasn't that bitingly salty water he assumed. He took just a few swallows, knowing too much would make him feel worse.

"What are you doing there, Jocelyn?" his sister Elianise asked.

"The water, here where the bottom is close, it's not so salty," Jocelyn observed cheerily. Quickly, Jacques passed an empty bottle Jocelyn's way and instructed him to fill it. Capfuls were taken by everyone, and the process repeated as long as the bottom remained close.

163

The last fill, made as the bottom receded again and their speed picked up, was undrinkable.

"Well, it was *something*," a man mused out loud. It was something.

XXVII.   October 16

We were very still. We did not move much. We had to save ourselves.

Gold from the Well
Jocelyn Apo

XXVIII.   October 17

Gold from the Well
Jocelyn Apo

XXIX.   October 18

Gold from the Well
Jocelyn Apo

XXX.   October 19

I don't think anything of this life on this earth is as strong as water.

Makenly made climbs to the top of the pole only twice a day now. They were slow and deliberate, draining him of the small bits of energy only a young healthy man would have in reserve under the circumstances. He did not recognize this task as a gift. He did not recognize that the ability to use his muscles twice a day gave him an advantage the other passengers were denied. No, he considered it a sacrifice made for the group, and made this perception very evident.

"Why would there be garbage dumped out here in the middle of the water?" he wondered aloud from the top of the pole. He was barely audible to the passengers as he faced northwest of their position.

Jacques considered this. "One of the luxury liners, maybe, though we haven't seen one for days," he theorized.

"No... Wait... the garbage is moving. It's moving..." he strained his eyes, blinking exaggeratedly to clear his mind as well as his vision. This declaration piqued the interest of a few more passengers than the idea of a garbage dumping, but most were still in the semi-hypnotic state the trip had imposed on them.

"No, oh mon Dieu! No! NOOOOOO!!!! Mon Dieu! Mon Dieu! It's PEOPLE!" Makenly was frozen at the top of the pole, but crossed himself.

"Jacques! What do we do? What do we do?! Their boat has broken apart. They are drowning!"

With this, all the passengers were jolted back into their weary bodies, and many sprung to their feet despite the danger of upsetting the boat.

Jocelyn, who always looked with blind faith to Jacques for the appropriate response, was distraught to see such ambivalence on the man's face. Jacques measured his response as he always did, and did not answer right away. But even if he had, he would be unheard over the screams of terror that had frantically broken days of near silence.

Then Jocelyn noted Jacques's lips moving, how he shook his head and turned away to face the path behind them.

"We must go," many shouted. "Save them!" said others. "They will sink us!" still another said. Every passenger aboard had an idea of what should be done, and none were presented as suggestion or potential. Every man and woman in their boat was compelled, as only life and death compels one, to either advance to the wreck or avoid it at all cost.

His superior height and great strength gave power to Makenly's voice to be heard over all the others. "Jacques! Get this boat over there NOW!!!!"

It was too much. It was too much. Jacques broke.

"If I could move this boat at my will, we would be in Miami! If I could move this boat at my will, we would be saved. This boat moves at God's will, as did THAT one!" he screamed, not even attempting to mask his sobs.

Jacques's words quieted everyone's voices, but not one of their emotions. Most of the passengers wept openly, and all showed clear signs of pleading with God. What were they bargaining for? Jocelyn asked himself this question as he prayed. "Please God, please take them home to you quickly. Please don't let the sharks come until you have carried them home. Please God. Please show your beautiful, bountiful mercy to these poor souls who are just like us, just seeking something better. Something simple, maybe. Take them home swiftly, Father. Take them home, I beg." He thought not of himself and his own safety. He thought of Maman, Marinath, Papa, Father Ojasma. He wondered if he would see them ever again, but Jocelyn dared not, DARED not ask for anything from God in this moment but for the delivery of these strangers.

But the fins came past their own boat quickly and moved on toward the wreckage. They were visible to more than just Jocelyn. Where there were 10 souls struggling, now there were eight. Now four…

Their trajectory carried them east to west, just as this boat had likely been traveling as well, but nearly a mile to the south of them. When they had finally closed the distance an hour later, and might have been able to pick up a passenger, there were none in sight. Only bits of wood floating, an article of clothing here and there. Jocelyn's boat was silent, again prayerful.

Anticipating the next wave of thoughts and emotions his charges were likely to experience, Jacques insisted, with great authority, "Our boat is sound. Not everyone thinks to varnish the inside. Not everyone thinks to cover the nail holes. Not everyone puts the extra coats of varnish on the outside. Not everyone gets varnish that will fight the salt. We built this boat to last. We did not rush. I say a prayer for all who did not feel they had the luxury of time, or perhaps did not possess the know-how to do it properly. But this boat will not be the reason we don't reach the United States, if we don't."

Judgment of Jacques for thinking of themselves at a time like this was reserved because, in essence, he *was* thinking of others – of 61 others who still drew breath, and happily squandered that precious breath to pray for the strangers who did not have the good fortune of enjoying Jacques's noble leadership.

XXXI.   October 20

A lot of people are a little bit emotional. They get a little bit emotional, a little bit upset. I remember one lady, I don't know what happened to her, usually that doesn't happen in Haiti, I've never seen it happen. She got up and for nothing she slapped her husband. I think maybe he say something she doesn't like. I think maybe he say we going to die. He got up and he slapped her back. They were very nice quiet people. They were both very nice people. We just don't know what happened.

Gold from the Well
Jocelyn Apo

XXXII.   October 21

We singing something, 'Se La Vi, Se La Vi'. It means I'm looking for life. I'm looking for life, and that's what I'm looking for, for life. I come from Cap Haitien, I'm going to the part in Haiti looking for life. And I say I come from this spot and I'm going to another spot looking for something better. That's how that whole song is. And it's also in French. 'C'est la vie. C'est la vie' mean this is the life. When you singing this is the life, that means something bad happened. Something bad happened. Whatever it is, it's not good.   And that was a moment we were very sad. Everybody very sad because we're not sure how long we're gonna be here in the water. And we're also nobody sure if we're gonna make it. Most not sure when we make it, if they gonna keep us or if they gonna take you back. And we know if we go back, if they keep us for a minute and they send us back to our country, we know we're gonna get in trouble.

Gold from the Well
Jocelyn Apo

XXXIII.   October 22

But I never doubt it. I never doubt God going to get me to the United States. When good happens to you, and bad is going to happen because this is the way God make it that some good thing going to happen, sometimes bad thing going to happen. And he with me all the time. I don't have nothing to worry.

Gold from the Well
Jocelyn Apo

XXXIV.   October 23

Another sunrise at their backs. Another day begun soaking wet.
Another day hungry. Another day thirsty. Another day of aching
muscles. Another day of skin so sunburned and taut that it cracked and
bled without warning. Another day of stench added to stench on top of
stench. Another day half in a daze from sleep deprivation. The brain
shuts down. If it had the fuel, *IF* it had fuel, perhaps it might try. But the
monotony of the struggle would seem to suggest it might not.

Makenly did not make his ascent up the pole. He had nearly lost
all motivation. Hours went by beyond the sunrise, and it was as though
he couldn't be bothered.

Adrift.

Adrift.

A luxury liner was observed west and far north of them. This one
didn't travel eastward as all the others did. Where might it be headed,
one or two passengers wondered.

Jocelyn turned wearily to Jacques, several positions away, and
said, "where do you think that luxury liner is heading? It travels south
instead of east."

Jacques roused himself from a morning nap after a rough night of navigation and strained his eyes. "Makenly!" he shouted suddenly. "Up the pole!"

Though Makenly's body had not changed its opinion on the notion of moving, his brain was awoken by the rare urgency in Jacques's voice. He ascended. Nothing happened quickly any more. But he spent all his reserves to climb.

"Describe the ship!" Jacques demanded. The passengers were now showing a great deal of interest. Looking around. Murmuring amongst themselves.

"It's different... It's not a luxury liner... There is a big red stripe... Some letters I can't make out... A large antennae at the top!" he barked each observation as he registered the differences between this ship and others they had seen.

Everyone aboard froze in amazement. What should they do? Without even blinking, they all followed its course from the north to a position due west of them, and then an odd thing happened. It stopped. It just stopped.

"I think it's the United States. I think it is their boat. They've seen us! They're coming!" Makenly shouted. But they did not come. They just stood, this magnificent ship, perhaps two miles away from their boat.

"They don't want to upset our boat with their giant wake!" Jacques reasoned.

"Go straight to them! Let's go straight to them!" one of Jocelyn's distant cousins shouted. Those who could reach over the side with any object that might serve as a paddle began urgently attempting to move the boat, lest the ship change its mind and begin to move again. The large stick was fished out of the bottom of the boat and likewise used for an inefficient paddle.

The boat, sound as the day it was completed, filled with 62 Haitians who believed in a better life, inched its way westward for half an hour. Despite storms, sharks, shipwrecks, nausea, despair, thirst, starvation, and fear of the unknown, these were the longest thirty minutes of their entire journey.

Gold from the Well
Jocelyn Apo

XXXV. Rescue

They drifted at last to the side of the enormous white ship. Several pale men leaned over the high deck, waving. They spoke, but were barely heard and not at all understood by the Haitians. A rope was dropped. One man gestured to tie the rope to the sail pole to anchor them to the side of the ship. Jocelyn began to attempt to climb up the rope. All the men on the upper deck vigorously gestured for him to stop.

Next, the Americans dropped down red life vests and gestured for each of the passengers to put them on, demonstrating how to tie them at the side. They complied. Finally, a rope ladder with wooden rungs was dropped, and once again Jocelyn was the first to grab at it. Jocelyn, and *all* the Haitians aboard had been raised to believe "men first." Of course, that said, he believed this had been his dream longer than anyone, and he justified the moment of selfishness to himself in this way.

Again, he was told something in a foreign language, but also in very clear signage that he must move aside for the young woman behind him. The Americans demonstrated climbing in mime, and one by one the women ascended the ladder.

Not a single Haitian questioned what fate awaited them above. They eagerly took their turns at the ladder. And when all the women had gone up, Jocelyn was, again, insistent on being first among the men to board.

As Jocelyn reached the railing over which the Americans had leaned, they continued to speak to him in English, but his puzzled expression reminded them to speak in gestures. They demonstrated that he should hold tight to the railing and step onto the deck. They shielding their faces from him just as they had each of the women (though this had been out of his line of sight from below). Just like Jacques with the Cubans, Jocelyn summoned a belly laugh and pinched his nose, indicating he was all too aware of his offense. One guard grinned, then ushered him to a gathering place on an expansive, wooden deck. Jocelyn's legs nearly gave out beneath him, but he was alive with adrenaline. Alive, praise God. Alive.

One by one the other men arrived, and the Haitians were utterly silent as they waited with great curiosity. Even before all had joined them, another guard emerged, from a nearby steel staircase, with a small cardboard box. Inside the box were small wrapped packages. Holding the box under an arm, the man removed one and clumsily demonstrated how to unwrap it, held the small white object to his nose, then appeared to rub it under his arm. With that, he approached the Haitians and passed out one bar of soap to each. When that had been accomplished, he walked back to the staircase and began to unwind a long coiled fire hose. As he returned to the Haitians, he turned his head back over his shoulder and let out a loud whistle to an unseen partner. Soon water was coming

186

with impressive force from the hose. He pointed to where they could "shower" and the water would run safely off the deck.

By now, Jacques had arrived and established himself as the leader. He bowed his head gratefully to the American, took the end of the hose, and tasted the water.

"It's good! It's fresh water!" he announced to the group. A roar went up. Everyone tightly gripped their respective bars of soap, and came up for a long, delicious drink of water before the showering commenced.

But commence it did. Jacques playfully sprayed the group who stood, by now, under a blazing midday sun. Once each person was wet, they went to fast work with their bars of soap lathering their heads, their clothes, and every crack and crevice under their clothes, right down to their hardened, heavy feet. One by one, they would cry out to be rinsed, then begin again until the soap was gone, in many cases. Some, after three or so washings, returned their bars of soap gingerly to the cardboard box. But not Jocelyn. He treasured this, the first bar of soap he had ever been given for his very own. He stashed it away in the waistband of his pants, and kept it a very long time as a symbol of his rescue and future prosperity.

As they dried rapidly in the baking sun, two more coast guards wearing white but soiled aprons emerged from the steel staircase carrying a large steel pot between them. They set it down on a low bench and beckoned the Haitians over. Pulling from a back pocket two small ladles, one of the men gestured for them to use them communally to serve themselves from the pot of soup. Instinctively recognizing that the pot would remain stationary given its enormity, the Haitians formed two lines at the soup. Each man and woman would take a ladleful, pass it, and go to the back of the line. Once again, Jocelyn pushed his way to the front.

"Oh, that is *good* soup!" he declared to the passengers who had more age and patience than he when he joined them at the back of the line. Each time he returned to the back, he crossed himself, then held his hands clasped together in childlike anticipation for his next ladleful. In the end, everyone had had what might amount to a small bowl of vegetable soup with a bit of noodles and meat, but after 19 days of hunger, and in some cases many more, it was a meal fit for a king.

Now the ocean was beautiful and welcoming to them. They stood on the front edge of the deck, feeling a fast wind blow over them as the ship moved at speeds they couldn't have imagined in their wooden boat, which remained tied in tow to the rear of the vessel.

"How long do you think it will be before we see the U.S.?" Jocelyn asked Jacques eagerly.

"That's very hard to say because I don't really know what part of Cuba it was we landed. We could still be very far away."

As though in answer, another coast guard appeared on the deck, now the middle of the afternoon, with a soccer ball. He offered it to the crowd to keep them occupied. A few kicked the ball around half-heartedly as they did not want to seem ungracious, but even the young were very weakened, and everyone was more interested in their mysterious future. Still, the appearance of an object with which to pass the time told the Haitians that it might be some time before they saw land.

As it grew dark, they were invited below deck where a television was playing. This was an entirely new experience to almost every man and woman aboard; its foreignness went far beyond the language barrier. Many stared in wonder, trying hard to work out in their heads what exactly they were being shown. And in their excitement, tried as they might on the spacious deck of the ship or the cozy hold below, none had enjoyed a moment of sleep all day.

Jocelyn was curious about the television, but not nearly as curious as he was about spotting land. After a short visit below, he returned to the leading edge of the ship, where he stared off to the north ahead of them. The sun continued to glow just below the horizon, off to the left, but soon only moonlight lit the deck. Jocelyn kept his eyes fixed on the line ahead of him where he knew the sky met the water. He grew tired, and noted that the temperature was dropping a much more comfortable range, but trained his focus on his would-be home. He barely dared to blink.

Perhaps an hour later, there came to be a glow ahead of them, not unlike the glow that the sun had left behind. At first it was just a sense that there was light ahead. Elianise came up and lay her hand gently on Jocelyn's back, stirring him from his intense focus.

"Land soon, little brother," she said gently.

"Yes. *Pays étranger*," Jocelyn replied, aware that Elianise had no idea of the extent of his private dream.

"Not for long…" she trailed off wistfully, implying it would no longer be a *foreign* land to them, with any luck. Jocelyn realized in that moment that he, likewise, did not know his sister's dreams. He barely knew his sister.

"We will not lose each other, Elianise," he said instinctively. He wrapped an arm around her, keeping his eyes on the horizon. The glow brightened in the short window of time they spoke.

"Do you see light?" he asked.

"Maybe. My eyes have played tricks on me," Elianise responded, only half joking. Jocelyn let out his second great laugh of the day, throwing his head back. "Let's watch together."

Jocelyn boasted excellent eye sight, so he was keenly aware when the glow became a distinct line of lights along the horizon. Then the line became individual lights studding the whole of the land before them.

Then the individual lights gained differing heights of their own as buildings of varying size emerged. Soon a mirror image of all these brilliant lights rippled on the waves ahead of them. It was glorious. Jocelyn and his many boatmates (who had slowly been trickling back up the deck outside of his notice) had never beheld so magnificent a sight. They were speechless. Breathless.

The land raced to them now, and the Haitians began to shiver with chill, exhaustion, and anticipation. Before they knew it they were docked and being guided down a walkway, where enormous buses awaited. The welcome they received in the United States, much like their welcome in Cuba, spoke of the thousands of their countrymen who had gone before them. But unlike Cuba where a select few came to their aid in trade, a small brigade greeted them and asked for nothing in return. Each man and woman received a light wool blanket, which they luxuriously wrapped around themselves. They were taken onto the buses and settled into the most comfortable, upholstered and cushioned seats that many, including Jocelyn, had ever had the pleasure of sitting in. None understood a word of English, nor had any idea where they were headed, but when the buses began to hum along from the Miami docks to the outer Florida Keys, the weary Haitians were lulled into a deep sleep at the wee hour of two in the morning.

Let me tell you. We don't make it to the United States on our own. The US Coast Guard gave us a ride to Miami. God blessed me and God loves me because, basically, we were lost. I'm coming from

191

the east going west, and the US Coast Guard was coming from the
north going south. And that's how they took us to Miami. We didn't
know where we were. I think they picked everybody up about 10:00
in the morning and we got to Miami Beach the next morning early.
We don't move. We got picked up at 10:00 and we got there at 2a.m.
in the morning. We were going to get lost because every morning we
don't move and we're so weak. After sliding so much because it got
wavy and we shoveled water outside and do a lot of different things,
we had no more energy left. We say God love us. Many times, all the
time, we say God love us. God love us because we think this country,
United States, is a good country. Any place that we go, we see a lot of
light. When we first came here in this country, first thing was really
impressed. We was impressed by it, every one of us, the light. There
was a lot of light. We never see so many lights. When you look on the
edge very far away, how you can see light on the water. And when
you look at it very far away, it seem like the light is lighting the sky.
The light lighting the sky. Because where the light is, the sky is bright
too. The sky looks bright. It's not dark. It was so beautiful, we all
stand up in the ship to see all the lights. It was so beautiful. God
bless American people. I say that with all my heart. Because
American people, they make a big difference in the whole entire
world. And I don't think they get enough credit. I don't think
everybody says 'thank you' to these people who make America the way
America is thanks to these people. If they wanted to keep this country

to themselves, they can do it, then today, I would not be here talking to you. God bless American people.

Gold from the Well
Jocelyn Apo

XXXVI. Refugees

At Key West, that's where they have a big camp – they don't call them camps – a big thing for refugees. Yeah. They've got a big thing here for refugees. When we got there, there was a big tent with a lot of cots or something you can lay down on. It was huge. Inside the camp where we were at, was as big as a Wal-Mart. It wasn't a house. It was something like they did for Haiti when we had the earthquake. They put a tent, but it's a huge one. Outside of those tents was a portable bathroom. Do you know those portable bathrooms like what they do on a concession? They've got a lot of them. Even today, I smell those and I love it. In Haiti no outhouse even. I had one built for my mother, but growing up, only outhouse if I am lucky. But those bathrooms, I see someone come and clean them out everyday. Every single day and they smell so clean I still love that smell. They have a tent like that for guys, and they have a tent like that for women in Key West.

In a continuation of their surreal experience, the sleepy refugees were promptly separated by sex and sent to sleep on a sea of cots, many of which were already occupied by Haitians and Cubans alike. The disruption in their sleep was only momentary; again, Jocelyn and his boatmates were so tremendously relieved by this pattern of hospitality that each stretched rapturously on his cot and returned to the deep sleep they had found at last on the buses.

The days that followed were a rife with cultural trial and error. The Haitians were brought cold milk for breakfast, which they refused out of belief that something must surely be wrong with milk that was cold. But generous servings of rice were ravenously consumed by the Haitians, and within a day or two a translator came in to learn what it was they *would* eat without suspicion. Each wave of refugees had their own unique set of idiosyncrasies, it seemed.

Previous inhabitants of the camp conveyed that much poking and prodding was to be expected. Medical examinations of every kind. Vaccination after vaccination. Dental hygiene attention. Each day a bus or two was filled to travel to downtown Miami where the refugees were seen, in rotation, by a litany of professionals. But in the intervening time, terrible boredom ensued.

Like so many other acts of nature, intimacy was something that Haitians were not brought up with any shame or shyness over. Now that their health was being quickly restored, and spirits were high, the Americans faced a particular challenge in keeping the population of the camp from experiencing an *internal* explosion. So, a few weeks into their stay, a very high wall was erected between the men's and women's tents with partial success in that endeavor. Even higher walls on the exterior of the camp fueled restlessness.

For three months, Jocelyn lived in the refugee camp, wondering every day what would come next, and when he could go and find work. Everyone worried whether the US would send them back to Haiti. One day, Jocelyn received a personal interview with a government official. A translator communicated for him, but there were gaps in what Jocelyn understood from this translator, so he was likewise not confident that his Creole sentiments were conveyed flawlessly.

I said I had to leave because I was suffering. It was very difficult and nothing to do. I was looking for a job and I wanted to help my mom, my dad and I wanted to have a better life for me and for my family. If they give me the opportunity, I promise them I can be somebody that I wanted to be for me and for my family. I left Haiti. I took the chance to come to American for a better life and a better future. I love to work. I worked hard when I was in my country. And when I came here, I would work the same, even more, if God blessed me and I could stay and find work to do. When I was back home, I worked hard and I love to work. That's all I did was work. And that's what I told them. I don't have any problem with the government in my country. A lot of people had problems with the government. If you have a problem with your government, this country here, they will keep you. They're not going to send you back because they know what they're going to do with you, they're going to kill you.

Not long after his interview, Jocelyn was taken with thirty or so other Haitian men to live at the Hotel Metropole in Miami Beach. There they were given intensive classes in English, fed generous meals, and permitted to enjoy the hotel pool. By helping out, Jocelyn ingratiated himself to the cook who had been hired to cater to them, thereby winning the extra portions his still-growing body needed. Jocelyn was so grateful for this treatment, but felt a burning desire to formally work for the lifestyle he was enjoying.

Jocelyn was placed in a room with a young man named Pedro who had been aboard his boat, but who, like Jocelyn, drew little or no attention to himself throughout the journey. Jocelyn noticed that between their English classes at a nearby Haitian school, Pedro would disappear for long stretches. Certain that God had sent Pedro to room with him by design, Jocelyn employed his trademark charm to get closer to Pedro.

"Hey brother, where do you go every day?" Jocelyn cheerfully asked Pedro one morning after offering him his extra roll at breakfast.

"I used to work for a man in Haiti called Fumet," Pedro responded simply. "He has a daughter, Nellie, here in Miami. I'm going to look for her."

Jocelyn couldn't help laughing at the idea that Pedro might find one woman in this great city when they didn't even know the language. "How are you going to do *that*?" Jocelyn wondered aloud.

"It's not so hard as you think," Pedro responded patiently. "In the Northeast there are lots and lots of Haitians, so they understand me. Also, they know each other. I've already been to one restaurant where the lady sort of hesitated when I asked if she knew Nellie, so I think maybe she does but she's just not telling me the truth."

"Really?" Jocelyn was astounded at Pedro's resourcefulness. He knew this was a guy to attach himself to. "How about I go with you? I can keep you company walking, and I can ask people, too, if they know Nellie Fumet, and, I'll tell you what, if I can get someone to give me a couple dollars, I'll give you a dollar!" Jocelyn reasoned.

"Sure, that's a good idea. Probably safer, too," said Pedro. They had been assigned immigration papers, and given strict instructions to have them stamped annually by the government. Whatever their place in the process of assimilating, they were advised to bring anyone whom would provide them employment to come to the hotel to disclose their intentions in writing. This was for their own protection, as was the urging that they never leave with anyone they didn't know. Jocelyn sensed that Pedro had arrived at the same conclusion as he: that he knew nobody in the United States so how would he ever find work? But Pedro *did* know this one person, and a woman at that, so this was the best plan they could envision to start their lives as Americans.

For several weeks, Jocelyn and Pedro logged close to 15 miles a day between the Hotel Metropole and Downtown Miami. Thanks to Pedro's instincts about the woman in the Haitian restaurant, and the pair's charming persistence with her, she finally became convinced that these two young men meant no harm to Nellie. Indeed, though Nellie first hung up on Pedro when he called, he was able on a subsequent dime to remind her of his service to her father, and that he was a worthy employee to have around. By the end of the week, Nellie came to the Hotel Metropole, signed for both Pedro and Jocelyn, and brought them to live with several other refugees on the floor of her large living room – palatial in comparison to anywhere either had lived – and quickly set to work introducing them to many prospective employers among her acquaintance. The two were brimming with gratitude.

XXXVII. Missteps

*When I lived with the lady, my first job was also in Miami
Beach because that's the only place I really knew for quite some time.
So I went over there and I saw some guy digging a swimming pool.
He had a machine and had all this stuff, but he just needed somebody
to take the extra dirt out for him. You know, when they dig it out,
sometimes they need somebody with a shovel to take the extra dirt out.
I worked for that guy for two weeks over there. Then after that two
weeks, I went over there to get paid and there's nowhere to find the
guy. The guy finished the job and he didn't pay me. He took off on
me. And I don't know how to ask him because there's no English. My
friend and I was on a bicycle when he was over there with me and
nowhere to find the guy. I wasn't happy at all. I needed that money.
The lady I was living with wanted me to give her a little money or
something.*

Nellie had been kind enough to provide housing, food, and
bicycles to Pedro, Jocelyn, and several other Haitian refugees. The men
slept on the floor, tended neatly to their things in the morning, and fixed
every leaky faucet, cracked dry wall, or burned lightbulb that could need
attention. The men joked that Nellie was as well protected as the
president with the revolving group of young men living under her roof.
One such man was Donald, who turned out also to be from Cap Haitian.

Jocelyn and Pedro became fast friends with him, enjoying his sense of humor.

Eager to repay Nellie's kindness, Jocelyn and Pedro were devastated when their first two weeks of labor was effectively stolen from them. They tried to express themselves to the new crew that came on to pour concrete for the residential pool they had helped dig, but it became very clear to them through a great deal of shoulder shrugging and waving that they were out of luck. It also became very clear why the government people at the Hotel Metropole were so insistent that they personally know prospective employers.

Riding their bicycles home, a policeman pulled up beside the two and gestured for them to pull over. Pedro and Jocelyn complied, but became agonizingly afraid. Being stopped by the police in their country was tantamount to a death sentence, especially if you had nothing with which to bribe them (which clearly the two had not).

As soon as the officers began asking questions, the two began to plead, "So sorry. No English. So, so sorry, no English." The officer continued in increasingly simple language, but neither Pedro nor Jocelyn had picked up enough at the Haitian school to comprehend the officer, and nerves were working hard against thet effort.

Finally, the officer reduced his inquiry to the simple demand, "Papers?" He cautiously pulled out his own identification, keeping a trained eye on the pair, pointed at it, and declared, "PAPERS?"

"Papers! Yes! Papers! Yes. So sorry. Yes! Papers!" the two fumbled in their pockets for the work cards they had been issued. They were overcome with relief that they understood the officer without a single blow having been exchanged. The officer looked over the identification, motioned for the two to stay where they were, and walked to his car where he used his radio to communicate with his precinct.

"What do you think?" Jocelyn demanded quietly of Pedro. "What's going to happen? Will they send us back? Do you think those pool people called about us?" He was dizzy with possible outcomes but remembered to cross himself and plead, "Please, Lord, please deliver us. Help this officer understand we are good, hard workers." Just then, a larger police vehicle pulled up behind them and the two really became scared.

The first officer returned to the two as a second officer exited the large vehicle behind them and flanked the two. Pedro and Jocelyn, independently, felt the strongest urge to run, but knew it would be a big mistake. By some miracle, they kept their feet firmly planted, and sweaty palms gripped the handlebars of their worn bicycles.

Officer number one began to gesture. Drive. House. Thumbs up. Pat on shoulder. Were the police going to take them home? Had they done something wrong, riding their bicycles on the road? The two were mystified. Again, Officer One gestered for them to stay, but gently eased the bicycle out of Jocelyn's grip. "Okay," he kept saying in a soothing voice. "Okay," as he took Pedro's bicycle as well. Officer Two finagled the two bicycles into his larger vehicle, and Officer One placed the men in the back seat of his car. Jocelyn and Pedro were completely dumbstruck, not even attempting to communicate with *one another* any longer.

After a prolonged two hours at a police station, and NOT Nellie's home, an interpreter was brought in. A white man approached them, and with the same soothing tone that the others had used, he inquired in Creole what had happened. Jocelyn was so relieved, he explained everything to the man. That they meant no harm to the swimming pool people, and went away as soon as they realized that the man they had dug for would not return. He explained that they didn't know the rules of the road, but they could ride their bicycles off to the side if needed. He insisted, pleaded, that he and Pedro wanted nothing more than to work and be American, and learn English, and pay Nellie rent, and learn to drive cars. Jocelyn then earned a pat on the shoulder from the interpreter as well. The man quickly explained to the officers in English all that Jocelyn had just poured out, and, miraculously, the two were let go. Just like that. Let go. The young men got back on their bicycles and rode home, carefully to the far right, exhausted from the day's drama.

Pedro and Jocelyn were almost home when Jocelyn, replaying the day's events over and over in his mind to be sure he could learn from it, realized that in his excitement to leave the police station, he had neglected to ask for his work card back. He began to shake.

"Pedro! PEDRO!" The two stopped right away. "I left my work card! Oh dearest Lord, what will happen? They will send me back. I will be killed. What shall we do?!" For the first time since he left his mother, Jocelyn began to weep. Seventeen days adrift on the Atlantic Ocean had not been enough to break him, but obstacle after obstacle in the land that would be his new home, that had held so much promise for him, became more than he could bear.

"We will go back, Jocelyn. It's okay. We'll go back, brother." Pedro's reassuring tone was all Jocelyn needed to collect himself, and remember to pray. God had spared his life on the water, he was surely going to continue his mercy for him. Jocelyn unapologetically wiped his damp face on the bottom of his shirt, and began his return trip to the police station.

Though the departure of the interpreter made it difficult for Jocelyn to explain to the evening shift what they were doing there, at last someone was able to understand the pair well enough to advise them where they could go in downtown Miami for a replacement work card when Jocelyn's was nowhere to be found. The very next day, Pedro and Jocelyn rode to the building where they had been directed, and not only did Jocelyn receive a new work card, but each also received a social security number and card which, they were advised, would help them for employment.

Staring at his new identification as they departed the building, looking at his own face in, really, only the second photo that had ever been taken of him, Jocelyn saw his father, Hachacha, distinctly. A flicker of homesickness came and went, and was replaced with an indelible determination to make his parents proud. Jocelyn gripped the cards tightly, shoved them way down into the pockets of the second-hand jeans he had been issued as a refugee, and rode home with a renewed sense of pride not only in where he was headed in life, but pride in where he had come from.

XXXVIII.   Adjusting

Then, I was working in a restaurant for $3.35 washing the dishes. And to me, that was a lot of money. Yes, $26.00 every two weeks in Haiti, but then when I came here, $3.35 per hour for washing dishes, that was a lot of money. I tell you that right now, that was a lot of money compared to where I was at. I was so happy for that and I thought that was a blessing. God bless me. And then after that, I paid a friend some money to work in construction for a little bit to get me in. That was $9 an hour. That was really lot of money, but they can't keep me because the job was finished. Then I worked putting telephone cable underground. That was $4.00 an hour. That was really a lot of money.

Four months went by. Pedro became consumed by fear of the unknown and returned to Haiti, though Jocelyn knew not how, nor ever spoke with him again. Jocelyn had good-paying jobs, and was able to repay Miss Nellie for her kindness. He was learning English, and took to heart the advice of the Haitian School teacher. "Don't learn any English in the street." It was slow going, but Jocelyn was catching on. He was strongly motivated by not wanting to find himself in the vulnerable position he had been in when his immigration papers were lost. He would show God that he was prepared to earn every blessing.

Jocelyn was able to save up money, especially as he and Donald had caught on to which restaurants threw out perfectly edible food around the same time they'd be leaving work. They often saved their appetites, and most days had plentiful bread from a bakery around the corner from Miss Nellie's house.

One morning as Jocelyn was leaving the Haitian school and mounting his bicycle to head to the restaurant where he washed dishes, he spied his cousin, Jacques, pacing the sidewalk outside the school.

"Jacques! *How are you?!*" he shouted. He was always eager to use his favorite phrase in English, and wanted to show off his progress to a man for whom he held so much respect.

The men embraced. "You look very well, Jocelyn! I believe you've grown taller!"

Jocelyn beamed. He threw back his head and laughed. "I eat well, here, cousin. Very well. And you! You look well also! Are you here taking classes?" Jocelyn gestured at the modest rented building.

"No, Jocelyn, I came to find you. Your sister, Elianise, actually paid me to find you. Her boyfriend can get you work cutting sugar for good money, and she misses you."

"Oh, yes! Wonderful! I will go right away! Thank you, Jacques! Are you cutting sugar too?" he asked, excited at the prospect of being reunited with these two family members.

Jacques became very grave. "No, Jocelyn, I'm going back."

Jocelyn braced dramatically, a gesture he had adopted with comedic intention, but was a difficult habit to break now. In this moment, however, it did demonstrate the authenticity of his shock. "What?" he finally managed to say.

"Jocelyn, who knows how long it will be before they *make* us go back – and to what end? I believe I can go and help others escape. I will start again. Build another boat. Make another journey. By then I will know better what it will be like for Haitians here."

After navigating the hiccup with his immigration papers, Jocelyn was in no doubt of his promising future in the United States. He felt God had shown him that he was here to stay. But his respect for Jacques in wanting to help others only deepened. He gave him a bear hug. "Bless you, Jacques. God bless you!"

The men walked together, catching up on the prior six months. Jocelyn placed the scrap of paper with his sister's phone number deep into his pocket. When time was running short, and he would have to ride to arrive at work on time, Jocelyn hugged his cousin again and wished him well. On his break from work, Jocelyn called the number Jacques had given him, and reached his sister. Elianise was excited to hear from him, and confirmed that her boyfriend, who was American, could get him a job cutting sugar cane, and Jocelyn could stay with them while he saved money. When he returned from his break, he gave his boss two weeks' notice, which he had learned was customary in the United States.

* * *

Cutting sugar cane was second nature to Jocelyn, though it took him time to get up to speed. Others were kind enough to help him with the rows he was expected to complete each hour, and soon enough he was able to repay that kindness as well. He lived briefly with Elianise and her boyfriend in Belle Glade, but wondered if leaving Nellie's was the right decision when the cane work came to an end. For weeks, Jocelyn had no work and grew dependent on his sister. With still only very little English, and now almost nobody he could call a friend, for the first time he grew despondent about his decision to come to the United States. He didn't know how he would return to Haiti, even if he wanted to – which he certainly didn't. Still, he thanked God every day to see the sun rise, and spent hours on foot or bicycle searching for work.

At last, his prayers were answered when Jocelyn ran into Donald once again.

"Are you still living with Nellie?" Jocelyn asked Donald, already sentimental about the kind woman's generosity.

"No, I share an apartment with five other guys over there in Avon Park, between Orlando and Key West. Mostly, we pick oranges – it's good money!" Donald told him.

"Can I come with you! I can pick oranges too!" Jocelyn asked with enthusiasm. He had no intention of letting Donald say no.

"You're a great guy, Jocelyn, but I'm just not sure…" Donald hesitated. "There's already six of us in the apartment – not really room for another."

"Oh, I can sleep on the floor!" Jocelyn offered genuinely. "And I'll still pay my share of the rent. I would love to come with you guys. I'll help with everything." Per usual, Jocelyn's charm was undeniable, so he embarked on the next chapter of his life in America. The seven traveled together for three years, first maintaining the apartment in Avon Park, and later in Miami, though their quest for work took them everywhere.

Gold from the Well
Jocelyn Apo

XXXIX. Adventures

In Florida, seven of us was living in a two-bedroom apartment and we was paying $125 a month. I picked oranges. I pick oranges in Florida, grapefruit and tangerine, and I cut the sugar cane, celery, tobacco. And I go with the other guys at a place called Immokalee in Florida. We picked watermelon. And then we went back to Key West, we picked tomatoes. They got a lot of tomatoes over there. In Florida, the Keys over there that way, they got a lot of plantation over there too, a lot of sugarcane. They got the thing where they make yellow sugar and white sugar. They got everything. And so, when I was over there picking tomatoes in Key West, and sometimes picking 200, sometimes 300, sometimes he pay 25 cents like a bucket, like a garbage can, a small one like you got by your office. And sometimes 35 cents, sometimes 50 cents we pick up. Sometimes I pick up 200. I start one and since the time I get there until time to go home, picking the tomatoes. And when the tomatoes finished, we go pick watermelon. When watermelon finished, if he have tangerine, we go pick tangerine in Florida. And if tangerine finished, we can do celery. We can cut celery. Right there in Florida they got tobacco. You can pick tobacco. And they got cotton. They got cotton and we pick cotton. They got cabbage. We cut cabbage. And they got potato. The machine pull the potato and we pick it up from the bin for them. We did that for quite some time. I do that in the different state too. Every time one job finished, we go to another one. Now, when this one was slow, we went someplace in the Key West area where

213

we picked lemon. Lemon, when we pick it, we have to cut it with the scissors. So they pay one bin 17 dollars. For two of us pick, very hard work, two of us pick one bin 17 dollars. It took us all day to do one bin. Those lemons, our fingers, our hand was hurting because the scissor, you only can use a scissor for so long. They don't want you to do it with your hands because they don't want juice twisted in the lemon. So the scissor make us tired. You know, that's why our hand cannot do. We only do one. And we split 17 dollars to two of us. And the next day, we're going back again to do another one.

We travel state to state. Sometimes we went to South Carolina, picking cucumbers, 35 cents a bucket cucumbers. Sometimes we got a lot, sometimes we don't have a lot. And tobacco. We go far in Georgia picking tobacco too. Those pay us 25 dollars a day for tobacco. That's different job, tobacco. Florida again, we plant the sugar cane. We cut sugar cane and we plant sugar cane. That would be 25 dollars a day planting sugar cane. When we go to Michigan; Grand Rapids, Benton Harbor, Oakley – we picked grapes, big black grapes, and they got apples. We picked apples. They got blueberries, they got raspberries. We picked raspberries in a little funny small cup to fill it out – 20 cents each one of them you fill. The grapes we had to cut – two dollars and 40 cents each one of them you fill. When I come in after I did all the rounds, even the Cubans, I used to go out with Cubans picking tomatoes too. I picked tomatoes 25

214

cents a bucket. Sometimes I picked up like two, three, four, five hundred buckets tomatoes, all big. And 20, 25 cents a bucket. Then after that, when those job is finished, we would go to Williamson, New York. Williamson, picking apples. We go to Sodus picking apples. We go to Wolcott. We did that season after season.

Sometimes, I swear God to you, God take my life right now, I'm not lying to you, sometimes we bring food and we're so focused on working, we don't eat it. We take it back home. We work all day, nonstop. And that's the reason why when you're coming for work, you can find a lot of people from Jamaica, Trinidad, Barbados and people from Mexico. They cannot come close to Haitian people really coming for work. Because every one of them, and I don't blame them, when it's time for lunch, for break, for breakfast or something, they gonna stop and eat, and we kept going, seven days. Way, way, way, way, way later. We stay way later. We begin to work six days, then after that, seven days again. All this time, we've been working seven days.

Now, seven of us lived together, we pay $125 for a two bedroom house to live in. Sometimes some of us sleep on the floor. Sometimes some of us sleep on the bed. We exchange. And then, when we cook, you know, seven days of the week, each day, one of us cooked. Tired or not, we cooked for everybody. If one of us got a doctor appointment, six of us would put together to pay him for that day he didn't come to work. Now, once when we went to Georgia to pick watermelon. Sometimes we go to Georgia, we pick watermelon.

215

We got to fill a whole truck for 75 dollars. So 75 dollars, and we split it to seven of us. Sometimes we can do two trucks, sometimes we can do three trucks in one day, watermelon, but it had to be full. We stayed for three months in the hotel. Each night, different of us go to the hotel and ask for a room. And then what we would do, we'd just put one mattress down and some of us, two people sleep in there and the rest of them sleep in there in the bed and some of them sleep right on the floor. And then we eat sardine and bread for three months. There was nowhere to cook. Sardine and bread, and a lot of juice and Coca-Cola, stuff like that, for three months.

One guy, his name was Patrick. He was a really popular guy. He know a little bit more English than us and he can read the map. He was here before I am. Patrick, and there was another guy named Jean-Claude, and Pierre, and there was Donald, there was another guy named OJ. My best buddy, he's an American guy. His name is Joe. Joe, he doesn't speak our language, but he doesn't have a place to sleep. Now we have a shower, but he doesn't like taking shower so we smell better than he does. We put him sleeping in our living room on the couch. Joe, especially when he passed gas, his smell take the whole living room. And then, when he work with his clothes, he worked in his clothes and come and sleep in it and pass gas at the same time with the door closed, and maybe drunk and snoring on the couch. So the next morning when you get up or if you come from *outside and you open the door, if you smell the whole house, you smell nothing but Joe. He was a nice guy. And you know, another thing too, we need him, because even if we're mumbling to him, he can figure it out better than the rest of the American people. But one day, one of those guys got so mad with Joe, and he got mad too this time, they put Joe out. It wasn't funny at all. They put Joe out because he doesn't want to take a shower. At the same time, we need Joe. We need Joe, because when we go to Winn-Dixie to buy something, if the lady say this is $19.95, we have no idea what she talking about. Joe had the truck. We met Joe in Florida. We were outside Miami in a little town called Avon Park. And then, he said, you know, the oranges are getting slow, let's go do something else. I'll drive you, so we paid him to drive. But later on, we're gonna buy a car. Seven of us gonna buy together, we're gonna buy a Thunderbird.*

When one thing finish, we go to another one. Well, while we were traveling, one day we got to Michigan. We got there two weeks early, and the camp where they put you sleep, there's no hot water, no stove, no nothing, but they have a well. They have a well where you can get the water. The water is cold, and we want to take shower. Sometimes what we do, we have to wrestle each other so we can get hot. You get off from work picking this stuff, apples and all the stuff we do, and we would just wrestle each other until we get hot. When we get hot, you go pick up the bucket of water then you take a shower

217

faster than anything you ever done before in your life. Oh man, if you never move fast, this water will make you move, I tell you. It's crazy.

When we were cutting the lemons, that's when we have an accident. Our friend fell down in the ditch of water because the guy who was driving, he didn't know there was a curve in front of him, so when he made the turn, he was going too fast so he fell down in the ditch of water. A big thing of water, the truck fell right down there. That thing has a lot of snake in it and a lot of alligator. They all was running away. And we tried to get out from the van, we can't come out. The guy we just passed, jumped in the water and come and break one window and pull us out.

And then after that, I was in Miami. At nighttime, with the same guy who have an accident when we was picking lemons. He was going too fast and he think he was gonna get the green light. The light turned red. Another car passed by, he hit the car like a T-bone. He hit the car. And it sent both of us into the side. One car go to the left, another car go to the right. Hit very hard. And then, my nose, it's almost like my nose and my head, the blood was all over the place on my body. But God helped me, I survived. That's the second accident with the same guy. Because he was speeding trying to get the light, that's what made it look like he was going fast, or it was the damage. It was a big mess. But I started going to the hospital and they fixed it and everything was all right.

218

While we work, we can talk. We can sing while we're working.
We're singing like some of those jazz. We had some of the jazz in
Haiti, the musician with the good music. Sometimes we sing their
song. There's a song that, and some of those guys, they were singing
like Christian songs. Some of those guys, they used to go quiet a little
bit, and they just humming. They'd be mumbling like that. But a lot of
time we're singing nice and loud. Sometimes we bring a tape from
Haiti we put together and we buy a radio. That was a big thing in
Florida. Sometimes people walking in the street, they got this big
radio in their hand.

I didn't find a church and I didn't look for one. I would just
pray at the place where I was at. I was asking God for direction,
because everything was kind of new and seemed to be confusing a
little bit. I don't wanna get into anything where I won't be able.
'Cause I know if I go to church, I will probably find some Haitian
people who will try to adopt me, and I don't know if I will be in good
hands with those type of people. I have no idea if it will be good or
bad, so I didn't go. Some of those places where we go to do migrant
work, some of those Christian people come right on the camp. They
pray for us. And sometimes, they come and get us. That happened in
Georgia too. And they pray for us and they come and ask us if we can
go to church with them. Sometimes they take us to church. Each
place we go, we go in the church for very little because we keep

traveling all the time. But we never forget to pray God for the direction.

XL.   Settling

Life had evolved into what Jocelyn had imagined it would be.
As a self-deprecating, mature gentleman, he would come to
affectionately refer to this period as his 'macho years.' He worked
hard. He had friends. He had seen Elianise from time to time. When
they were in Miami, they would go downtown where he taught
himself to dance by watching the lively Cubans, whose rich culture
flavored the colorful days and the bright evenings. The *Bachata*. The
Cha Cha Cha. The *Merengue*. *SALSA*! Jocelyn enjoyed a small
elegant wardrobe, sweet smelling cologne that pushed out his
memories of always being dirty, and for the first time in his life, he
actively pursued women. He thought often of Maman and the rest of
his family, but had no way to contact them, or, worse yet, share his
prosperity. He still had visions of having his own home and one day
visiting Haiti again, but for Jocelyn, both remained distant dreams.

One autumn day in 1984, the guys were heading out to pick
oranges, but Jocelyn declined to join them. He was filled with the
sensation that took hold on occasion: God was going to reveal a plan
to him. So, while they loaded up the Thunderbird and drove away,
Jocelyn found his favorite Haitian Christian station on the shared
radio, and set about cleaning the apartment.

"Are you a legal resident looking to make a change? The U.S.
government is offering free relocation service, job placement, and a

small stipend while you get settled in a new city. Cincinnati, Ohio. Pittsburgh, Pennsylvania. Indianapolis, Indiana. Rochester, New York. Newark, New Jersey..."

Jocelyn froze and perked his ears. He knew many of these cities. Working God's land had been good to him, but he knew he could only work so physically for so long. What sort of job might they be offering? Surely they wouldn't bother to advertise like this for mere dish washing. His mind spun.

"...These are just a few of the beautiful cities in the eastern states opening their doors to new immigrants..."

On December 9, 1984, Jocelyn boarded his first plane ever in Florida and landed, that very same day, in Rochester, New York. Between the foreign sensations from without, and the sea of questions from within, he was a bundle of nerves the whole flight. Jocelyn arrived to a snowy day wearing shorts and bright white sneakers, and was greeted by an English-speaking Haitian man who held up a simple sign, "Jocelyn Apo," and warmly greeted him. Though Jocelyn knew he was expected, this vision was, to him, a clear sign from God.

* * *

I come in the program. I come with the program where they're gonna give me place to live. They're gonna give me $75 a month. I'll

be rich with that money. $75, they give me place to sleep and they
give me $75 so I can eat, and they're gonna look for a job for me. It
can't be any better. I feel like a rich man. Yeah.

* * *

The man at the airport was named Joseph. Joseph, himself a
Haitian immigrant, worked for the agency that would help Jocelyn
find work. He drove Jocelyn to his first Rochester home at 737 Bay
Street, where he would reside for his first two years in Rochester.
Joseph walked Jocelyn into the home and introduced him to the three
others Haitians residing there, as well as the home's owner, Jabuel,
and his wife. Jocelyn was immediately reminded of Nellie's house,
and a happy familiarity washed over him.

His first few weeks were terribly restless. Anytime anyone
was going anywhere, be it the the grocery store, hardware store, or
even just the post office, Jocelyn would beg, "Take me with you!" as
he hated to be alone with nothing to do. All the other residents had
jobs, but at different times of the day, so despite the winter weather he
could generally stay busy by hounding them in turn.

On his second Saturday, he found one of his fellow residents,
Morris, getting dressed up. "Where you going, my friend?" Jocelyn
inquired enthusiastically.

"Oh, I'm going dancing, brother!" Morris grinned ear to ear, and demonstrated a few steps of the cha-cha as he kept his gaze in the mirror, ensuring a close shave with his electric razor. Jocelyn lit up.

"Oh, I LOVE to dance. I can go with you?" he pled shamelessly, echoing Morris's cha cha steps. He spun for effect, fondly remembering so many warm nights in Miami.

"Yes, but we must walk a few miles and you have no boots!" Morris chastised him.

"Oh, that's okay, my feet will be warm, knowing they are going dancing!" Jocelyn shouted as he practically skipped to his own room to find his best pair of pants and a button down shirt to wear.

It was a long, cold walk of two miles, but many lights for the holidays made the trip pleasant. Inside the club, which specialized in the kind of Spanish music Jocelyn had come to love, it was warm and wonderful. Women and the occasional brave man packed the dance floor.

"Now listen, if you ask a girl to dance, make sure you know what you're doing," Morris advised, "or she's going to tell all her friends you're no good!" Jocelyn laughed. He was confident in his dancing ability, but nursed a soda water at the bar for quite some time to feed his confidence. Sure enough, when a *Salsa* song played, the dance floor nearly cleared except for a small handful of people, and what he saw was very different from the *Salsa* steps *he* knew. That was to say, they moved much faster than he ever had in Miami. He took many mental notes.

When the *Salsa* was over, and a *Merengue* song came on, Jocelyn finally screwed up his courage and approached a young woman he had been watching. She seemed to know the steps but not take it too seriously, and accepted Jocelyn's invitation back to the floor. Here Jocelyn thought he knew what he was doing, but quickly realized even the faithful old *Merengue* differed somewhat from what he was used to. Three times he stepped on the poor girl's feet, so it was no surprise to him that she made excuses to return to her friends after their dance. Jocelyn resolved to work on his steps in the privacy of his room before they returned to the club.

* * *

Two weeks later, once Joseph had gotten a feel for how industrious Jocelyn was around Jabuel's house, he introduced him to a friend of the agency, Joe Bujak. Joe contracted with the Blossom Nursing Home to clean the floors. On Joseph's recommendation, Joe gave Jocelyn a job right away. Jocelyn was thrilled that he would have an *indoor* job, especially as the winter wore on, growing even colder.

"We got to celebrate!" Jocelyn urged Morris, eager to return to the Spanish club, though not excited about the cold trek. "How about we offer buy Jabuel drinks. Maybe he drive us in his car?" Jocelyn proposed.

"I like the way you think!" Morris teased Jocelyn. Luckily for them, Jabuel accepted the invitation, and that Friday night they were headed back to the club. Jocelyn was astonished at the moves Jabuel, an older gentleman, broke out. He watched him attentively, still a little hesitant to ask any girls to dance, and picked up even more from the obviously seasoned dancer. As the beat drummed in his ears, warmth radiating off of the strangers around him, Jocelyn contemplated a new job, a new home, new friends. Though he still missed Maman every moment, he was filled with promise for the future in a way that migrant work had never offered.

XLI. Blossom

I take the bus to Blossom. That's how I get to work. But, you know, I go the wrong way. I don't know if I go on the one on the right or the left. Then I see I'm going the wrong way, and I don't know how to ring to tell the guy, the driver, I need to get off. Many times I do that. Sometimes I get off and just run so I won't be too late. But I do a good job so I keep that job even if I was late a few times in the beginning.

I was a floor man. My job is to do the floor. I strip the floor. I washed the floor. And I buff 'em. I mop 'em. And I mop the room. And the hallway, I make them look shiny. And that was my job, but I ended up doing more, a lot more. I get involved more than I'm supposed to be doing. Every time they have something, they called 'In Service,' I wanted to be there. I wanted to learn. I'm learning without training. Some of those old people, they have no idea their food is right there. And their eyes are wide open. They don't even eat. This is the way it worked sometimes in this country, a lot of young, they don't have the respect for older. It wasn't like that for me when I was coming up. If you need some information, it is your best bet to go to the older people. Those are the ones who are gonna give you the answer you're looking for. The young won't have no idea. No idea. They haven't been there yet, you know.

* * *

Jocelyn's floors were the cleanest in the whole building. He learned quickly, and knew the only way to demonstrate how invaluable an employee he could be was to do his job well. Or so he thought. Joy oozed out of Jocelyn wherever he went, and there is nowhere better in the world to notice the specialness of such a quality than a nursing home. He whistled while he mopped. In time, as his English and his confidence developed, all the residents became "Princess," or "Captain." "Beautiful," or "Lady Killer." Smiles became more contagious at Blossom than the common cold, and everyone recognized Jocelyn as the root of this epidemic.

"Why you not eat, Princess?" he would coax lonely residents he found slumped over their meals. "I dance for you, you eat, Princess?" he would bargain. Next thing you know, Jocelyn and his mop were performing the *Merengue* in the halls, and 'Princess' was eating heartily.

Mr. Jones might be resisting his therapists for a morning constitutional through the building. "Watch out, Lady Killer! You don't exercise, they make you do this!" Without missing a beat, Jocelyn would be standing on his hands, doing pushups with his now strongly developed legs effortlessly suspended over him.

* * *

I have a wonderful relationship with a lady named Loretta.
And she was 100 years old. And she's very little. And so beautiful.
And sometimes she liked to walk around a little bit with her cane. She
got a thing so she can balance a little bit. And when she dropped
something, sometimes I'm on the other side of the hallway, and I saw
she dropped it, and I'd run, run, run, run, run, run. I run very fast,
and I say, 'I'm coming Loretta. I'm almost here. I'm almost here.' So
you know, she'd drop it right there by her feet. I come from all the
way to the end and I run very fast, and I'd get it before she can bend
down and get it. And she'd laugh. Yeah. She'd laugh.

* * *

The only struggle anyone had with Jocelyn was remembering or pronouncing his beautiful name.

"Zho SLEHN," he would patiently remind the residents in his exotic accent when, over and over, he would be asked his name. He understood that most of these elderly people had probably never known anyone with this foreign name, and that he was difficult to understand to begin with. "Je m'appelle Zho SLEHN."

His supervisor, Lize, heard him as she passed by one day, and took him aside.

"What would you think of me calling you 'Joshy', or 'Josh', Jocelyn?"

229

There was nothing condescending in her tone, so Jocelyn embraced this idea. "Oh yeah! Das good! American name for Jocelyn," he mused aloud. "Joshy. Josh," he tried it on for himself.

Lize reached up to pat this powerhouse of a man (who proudly owned his full six feet, and a spare inch) on his arm.

"Good grief, Joshy, those are some arms!" she teased.

"Oh, yah, Joshy eat very good now, and work hard!" he accepted her compliment, smiling widely, even flexing dramatically for the laugh he knew he would get.

"Keep working hard!" she smiled as she returned to her office.

* * *

I move out from that house and got my own apartment. But I always living very close to downtown. I like it, it's more comfortable, I know the area better, I can pop up the expressway once I drive, I can go right there, Walmart. Bam, everywhere. Long time ago there used to be a store called "Gold Circle." I used to work for them. I used to give them my phone number. When the truck is coming, 18-wheeler, they have a lot of heavy stuff. They want somebody to come and unload the truck. One point, I ride my bicycle on a nice day when I have free time. Because Blossom, I work two weeks straight and I got four days off. I used to ride my bicycle, and I put my name and

my phone number, and nationality I am, I say, 'I can do it better for
cheap' and I put in people's mailbox. And I put around Blossom
neighborhood, and I tell them I work in the nursing home. For a
good amount, I don't have a TV, I don't have a phone. I have a pager
maybe 1990-something. After that, there was a company called
Rochester telephone and I had someone helped me get a phone at my
house. But I go to pay phone in the rain, the snow.

In the off hours, my favorite place to go was so close by.
Tops. Tops is at Blossom and Winton Road. My favorite place. They
got a big museum right there too. There's a lot of stuff I don't like. I
can't eat them . I begin to cook some rice. When I was back home,
when women cooking in the kitchen, they don't want a guy to be there.
But you know, right now at that time, I can cook, but I don't learn it
from anybody. I do not know how to go to the restaurant because I
cannot order from the menu. Even though I been here quite some
time, I can't read the menu. Now, if I go to Tops, I been here a little
bit now, I know numbers, I know exactly how much something cost
and I can easily get it, but I cannot go to McDonalds or Wendy's to
get something, because at the time they don't have a number. Those
number things for meals, they just come up. When I go to work I cook
some rice and bean, mix in vegetables, and I take it and eat it. I never
eat dessert. Even today, I never eat dessert. If I'm hungry, you give
me cake, you give me cookie or something, I'm eating it right now.
But when I finish eating a meal, no such thing, dessert. Never

231

thinking about it in my life. And I go to the gym. At one time I could bench 300. Now just 250. But when I was young and handsome, had hair on my head... 300.

They have a club they call 2001 all the way down in Chili. I don't have a car. There was another club they call City Limit. That's right there in Chili too. Those are American Club. Back then, when you meet a lady, that's where you take them. Everybody dress up nice. In Henrietta they got a club they call 747. In the city they got another one they call 27. That's the only thing I was doing on weekends.

XLII. Construction

Joe passed away, but Blossom retained Jocelyn and other workers to clean the floors. He loved his job at Blossom, but Jocelyn, 'Josh', began to suspect that he could be more successful returning to construction. So, with some regret, he left Blossom after four years to join a construction company which was adding on to the George Eastman House in a fashionable neighborhood downtown, as well as other large projects.

For the first year, Josh would hitch a ride with the other workers, giving them gas money whenever they requested it. He attended classes at the Family Learning Center on Hart Street in pursuit of enough knowledge to earn a driver's license. Evening classes were difficult for him, but Josh was undeterred. He was discovering that, just as in Miami, Haitian people in Rochester came to know other Haitian people. In this way, he came across Jean-Claude, with whom he had traveled the country doing farm work. Jean-Claude had landed in Rochester even before Josh, and his English was progressing remarkably.

"It's tough, the reading!" Josh lamented to Jean-Claude one summer evening as he waited for a bus on Hart Street. "How'd you do it?"

"I got a *tutor*, that's a teacher who just work with YOU," Jean-Claude shared.

"Can you get me a tutor?" Josh asked sheepishly. Jean-Claude was a decent guy, but someone Josh wasn't quite sure had ever taken a real shine to him.

"Yeah, you just sign up at the front desk there at the Center, Jocelyn! My lady's name is Mrs. Newton. You ask for her. She's good!"

"Oh, good, okay, I'll do that!" Josh said, relieved that Jean-Claude didn't take the opportunity to chastise him.

* * *

Mrs. Newton is the most wonderful person I ever met my whole life. She has that gift God give to her. At that time she at least 70 years old, her husband close to 80. They done working. They retired. They stay home. And they so kind! She work as tutor just volunteer! She taught me a lot. How to write a check. That's very important. She taught me about this country, about laws, you can get into trouble. She taught me math. She taught me to read! Like right now, I have to say thanks to her every time I read a text. I go to her once a week for long time. She give me homework. Right now I feel like I was very hungry to learn because I really wanted to get everything going for me.

I don't have a GED. I never been thinking of school. Even back home, when we started, we never finish anything. When I was in Florida I do some too, but my life is all moving, moving, moving, moving. When I come here, I went to 30 Hart Street. Family Learning Center. I was there for long time. I was knowing a little bit, and Mrs. Newton helped me learn the rest. Pretty soon, I get a driver license.

* * *

Josh's first car was an $800 Chevrolet. It got him from point A to point B, but not without plenty of hassle. Earning eight dollars an hour in construction was certainly better than the four dollars an hour he made at Blossom, but he seemed to be sinking a lot of that money into parts. Then one day, his worksite was visited by the Department of Labor. Josh could not suppress his curiosity.

"How much are you paying these guys?" he heard the agent demand of his foreman. The foreman quickly moved the man away from the other workers, who began to buzz. Josh heard a guy, Charlie, talking to a few of the guys.

"It was me, man. Union says we should be getting $17 an hour. But I knew I'd be the first to go if I went to management. We're going to get what we deserve now!"

Josh took all this in and kept his head down. Three weeks later, each of the workers received a check compensating them with

235

back pay. Josh had never seen a check this large made out to him in all his life. Gleefully, he sold his car and found himself a black Trans Am. It had a "Z top" and headlights that opened and closed. Josh had arrived. And arrive *in style* is what he would do weekends at the clubs.

* * *

At that time I was working in construction for three years. As I was in construction, I just love to go out. I met people I work with who want to go out, but sometimes they too tired. But I don't let the too tired slow me down. We would go out… we work construction seven days! I was working for a guy, Dave Richards. I worked for him for a long time. After that, we go to a club called Calabash, and one called La Freak and the people begin to fight. When they begin to fight, they begin to shoot, and what I did… they began to close some of those clubs, I give my back to American club. I give my back completely to American club and I give my attention to Spanish club. And that's when I become very good and dancing and teaching people and I go all the way to Buffalo, club called La Lunas, to perform. I go to Darien Lake, we make commercial performing. Public Market. And I was in news at the Public Market. One time in an early morning show we did something for channel 13 in Henrietta at the news station. This is the time when I began teach people, do private classes. And then last year, every Saturday, I go people's house, I teach them to do Salsa.

But the guys in construction, they were pretty tough. At the time, I was new, and they was older and had been there before. And some of those language they was talking, I wasn't familiar with them. Well, it kind of make me feel a little bit uncomfortable. But sometimes I tried to block my ears because I really need that job. And so, I put up with the mess for quite some time. I stayed there and worked with them for two years. For two years, I worked with them. And when I tell 'em, OK, I can't do this no more. I tell 'em I'm gonna give 'em two weeks' notice. I can't do it no more, I'm gonna have to go.' And they don't like for me to go. They were kind of upset because I was really, really good worker.

* * *

Josh worked for a few months through a temporary employment agency, but felt God guiding him to return to Blossom. Keith, who had known of Jocelyn, 'Josh', and the impact he had on the residents, had come up through the ranks and was now in charge of hiring. Not only was Josh offered his job back on the spot, but he learned that Keith had been looking for a way to get a hold of him for some time. Josh picked up right where he had left off, doing an excellent job of cleaning, and a spectacular job of improving morale. Twice a year, at Keith's urging, Josh rented a tux, invited other

237

Rochesterians he had made friends with downtown, and put on a dancing show for the residents. He also badgered the Blossom employees he came to know well to help them out around their homes for whatever they might pay. Cleaning. Painting. Gardening. He would do anything for more work. Work to show God that he would never cease to earn his blessings. Work to fill his bucket with gold.

XLIII.   Maman

Work with the elderly in the United States brought Maman to mind every day for Jocelyn. By now she was probably an old woman in a country where the standard of living was not kind on the aging. *If* he was lucky, he thought. *If* Maman was still living. But he felt her spirit inside himself every day and couldn't believe God would not have made it clear to him if He had called her home. Jocelyn's ears rang every night, telling him Maman was praying for him.

It had been ten years at least since he laid eyes on her. Since he heard her voice. He could only imagine, now, how she smelled, in much the same way he used to imagine his *pays étranger*. Dreams of Maman came with increasing frequency. He would see her smiling face in the bright Haitian sun. Though he had not yet earned his citizenship, nor the confidence it might have given him to risk going back, he set a plan in motion to return, telling no one but the agency that insured the legality of his travel from and back into the U.S.

Boarding the second plane of his life, Jocelyn departed Rochester, changed planes in his old city of Miami, and landed, shaking, in Port-au-Prince. He realized that despite how extensively he could navigate his comparatively huge new country, he was ignorant about the luxury of hired transportation in this small homeland, and was certainly less inclined to trust strangers. He felt his best chances of making the four hour trip to Cap Haitien safely would be a private taxi. So, he settled on a price with the driver and they set out at dusk. The trip was uneventful after Jocelyn stood up aggressively to the driver when the man tried to take another passenger. He wasn't sure what inspired him to do so – in the United States he was always deferential. But the hardness of a suspicious culture returned to him naturally – easily, even, now that he was a grown man with plentiful cash in his pocket.

When I get to my mother's house, I think it was maybe 12:30, one o'clock. They sleeping. Hard part is, I don't know how to find her. It's dark, I don't remember. Plus, she move. But lucky for me, sometimes people, at nighttime, they walk by themself. So I tell the taxi guy stop. I heard one voice and I say, "Oh, that's Jacques!" Not my cousin Jacques, but different Jacques I know growing up. I say, "Hey, do you know where Amancia live?" He say, "No, but let me go to this house and ask." We knock at couple houses, they all tell us which way. Everybody who do that, I give them a couple dollars.

"Amancia?" Jocelyn and Jacques inquired softly, musically even, outside Maman's house.

"Yes, it's Amancia," Maman answered curiously. "Who's that?" The direction of her voice told Jocelyn she was moving to the door.

He spoke softly. "Don't be scared. It's your son. I'm your son."

She came out into the moonlight. "My baby? MY BABY?" she cried. She touched his face and took in this grown man. "Amos!" She threw her arms around him and sobbed. "Amos, they told me you were dead but I could never believe it. I never believed it. I prayed for you every day, Amos…"

"I know, Maman," Jocelyn could barely managed. "And I have prayed for you. And God has brought us together again." They embraced and felt the miracle of reuniting wash over them.

Jocelyn spent that night in the home with Maman, but both felt he would be safer in a hotel for the remainder of his visit. Amancia would sit and listen for hours while her strapping son renewed all her pride with colorful stories about all he had done since their separation. At her invitation, many of the people he had known growing up came and went from the hotel to see him and hear his stories. To each, these people who had been his elders, giving him a penny here and there as a child, he gave a few dollars. He felt a dark sort of embarrassment that he could not give more, yet understood that the gesture, and any little luxury he could provide, was appreciated.

Upon his departure the following week, Jocelyn made a solemn promise to Maman, whom he was able to leave with *more* than a few dollars:

"I will take care of you for the rest of your life, Maman. I will be back again soon, and I will send money now that I know it will reach you."

"And I will pray for you *every* day, Amos. Every single day."

"Me too, Maman," he hugged her with so much more joy than he had felt leaving her ten years before.

* * *

After that I go back again, I didn't tell her I'm coming. This time I take a bus from the airport. It take a long time. Then a taxi to my mother's house. When I go back there, my mother is carrying this thing over her head. As she was walking I can see who she is behind her back. And then I tell the taxi, "When you get to that lady right there, you stop." And the taxi stop, and I went over her head, I pick up that thing, put it in the trunk of the car and said, "Come on, Maman, get in, let's go!" She was so shocked. She was SO shocked, and she was so happy! Every time I surprise her. I'm a very secretive person. Whatever happen, it should stay between me and God.

* * *

Over the years, Jocelyn made many trips home, visiting his sisters as long as they were living, as well as their families.

Marinath's daughter, Edelime, took Amancia in when she became too old and frail to work, eventually losing her vision. But Jocelyn made a pact with Edelime. "You take care of Grand Maman, and I will take care of your family." Through the years he had a well installed, an outhouse built, provided them with a cell phone on which he would call Maman often, a generator, and money for food whenever it was needed.

Gold from the Well
Jocelyn Apo

XLIV. Suzanne

Suzanne Robinson's father – his wife, Suzanne's mama, was there at Blossom and he come and take care of his wife all the time. And then when Susan Robinson come and see me over there all the time, and her father told her about me, how good I am. You know, the floor looking good. And I always help him with his wife, if he wanted to pick her up. Sometimes he come and he brush her mouth off. He do all kind of stuff for her. And if he need my help for whatever he may need, I'm helping him. And then, I begin to go to Suzanne Robinson's father's house, work in his yard and then also clean house for him. Now, where I was working over there, I was working over at her house, too, sometimes, cleaning her house. Yes. I was working at her house. Every two weeks, I go over there and mop the floor. I clean the toilet. And basically, that's it. With a vacuum and stuff like that, because the house is really clean, you know. I was still working at Blossom. And then, after that, after a while, Suzanne Robinson coming from the elevator, and she said to me, 'you know, I'm gonna get you a job where I work.' And she did.

Visits to Blossom Nursing Home were fraught with emotional ambivalence for Suzanne. It pained her to watch her mother deteriorate, though her father's daily attention to her was touching. "This is how I make love to your mother now," he would tell his children. The staff was almost always kind and friendly, which

245

helped to validate their choice of Blossom in Mother's twilight, but one face stood out as a prince among men.

Jocelyn, or "Josh" as she noticed some of the staff and residents calling him, was a bubbly young man whose richly toned face always wore a broad smile. She knew it was a genuine happiness because she could think of many occasions when she happened around a corner, spied 'Jozzy,' as she liked to call him, just smiling to himself as he buffed the spotless floors. Watching Mother light up when he poked his head in to say musically, "Good morning, How ARE you today, Princess?" in that beautiful accent cheered Suzanne immeasurably. He had proven himself a hard worker at her parent's home, as well, and Suzanne felt compelled to do something for this man who seemed an endless source of energy and mirth.

"I come work for you, Miss Suzanne. You work very hard at that school. Teachers SO important! How about I come clean your house?" Jozzy had insisted more than once. Eventually she relented, not entirely because she was in need of the help, but he spoke often of wanting to help his family in Haiti, and she had so much admiration for his work ethic, motive, and ambition.

"Okay, Jozzy, do you know where Pittsford is?"

Jocelyn grinned widely. "Yeah, Pittsford, that's… that's… wait, I been to Pittsford before when I work in construction, but maybe you just remind me…"

Teaching in a middle school had honed Suzanne's skill for detecting baloney. Still, she knew a certain amount of improvisation was central to Jocelyn's resourcefulness and therefore his advancement in the world. She was eager to pave the way.

"I don't want you getting lost, Jozzy. Let's see… Do you know where Monroe Avenue is?"

"Oh sure, Monroe Avenue! That downtown. That in Pittsford too?" Jocelyn beamed.

"Well, Monroe Avenue comes all the way into Pittsford, yes. How about if you take Monroe Avenue south until you go under highway 590, and then you'll see a McDonalds on the left about half a mile away. Can you meet me there at 9:00 am next Saturday?"

"Yes, yes, I do that!" Jozzy returned excitedly. Suzanne would have been dubious, like facing the waitress who doesn't write down your order, but she knew from Jocelyn's work at her parents' that he committed times, places, directions to memory.

Over the coming weeks and months, Suzanne would meet him at the same location, then further out, at the Farm Stand on East Avenue until Jozzy could find her home effortlessly. She noticed

247

how easily he acclimated to sterile Pittsford, chatting with neighbors when he was helping with yard work, and even striking up future employment opportunities with them. It got Suzanne thinking. After a candid conversation with the young man about his benefits at Blossom, and an inquiry at Pittsford Middle School, she floated Jozzy a proposition when she next saw him in his glistening hallways.

"You know, Jozzy, Pittsford schools offer great benefits, including sick days, vacation days, and a retirement plan. I can tell you're a man who thinks a lot about the future. You could make a little more per hour *and* be saving for retirement if you came to work at Pittsford Middle School where I work."

"Oh really?" Jocelyn's curiosity was piqued. He received more and more offers every day of small, odd jobs, but this was a real career step.

"Absolutely. You are so great with the residents here, and I know how much you'll be missed, but, you know, I think you'll discover you like working around kids just as much," she promised. "I could even help you with your application, Jozzy."

"You would do that, Miss Suzanne? Thank you!" Jocelyn was touched.

"Jozzy, I think you are going to discover that the people in Pittsford will be very happy to give you opportunities, you are such a sweet man to have around." She walked to see her mother after setting a time when they could visit the Pittsford Central School District together.

* * *

After Jocelyn was offered an interview, the real work came.

"Hey Jozzy, you told me that you had help getting this job when you were new to Rochester. Have you ever sat for a job interview?" Suzanne posed gently, fearing she already knew the answer.

"No, no interview exactly," Jocelyn reflected.

"Okay, Alan and I are going to help you prepare, young man. I don't want to make you nervous, but how you present yourself is very important."

Jocelyn looked down at himself and considered his appearance as he stood in the hallway at Blossom. He took such pride in always being clean, smelling good. Suzanne read his mind.

"I *know* you will make a FINE impression, but there are just some subtleties to interviewing. For example…" She paused at length, waiting to see if he would meet her eyes, rather than staring at the top of his mop handle. Only after she waited at length and he grew curious did he look into her eyes. "There you go! You must always look *in the eyes* of the interviewer!"

"That's not respectful how I grew up," Jocelyn lamented.

"I get it. You want to be respectful. That's good. But Jozzy, what if I were to tell you that if you don't look someone in the eye in the United States, they might think you're dishonest. That you're not telling the truth."

"What?" Jocelyn demanded, mortified.

"Yes, Jozzy. This is very important. And you have to be able to brag about yourself a little more!" She gave him a little shove, knowing how this would come across to so humble a man.

"What do you mean, 'brag'?" Jocelyn knew well the meaning of the word, but could not imagine that a prospective employer would value bragging. His mother had always taught him to let his good work speak for itself.

"I am not kidding, Jozzy. But, you know, find a balance. 'What are you good at?' 'Well, sir, I'm told that my floors are the cleanest at Blossom, and I stay on top of the trash so well that the place smells more like a school than a nursing home,' see what I mean?" she offered.

"Sure, yeah, I'll think about that," Jocelyn pondered, his eyes back on his mop.

"Eyes!" she demanded. They laughed.

"Okay, you're going to do more than think about it. This Saturday, and Sunday, Monday, whatever it takes – Alan is going to give you practice interviewing. I'm sorry to be bossy about it, but you know I have your best interest at heart," she beamed, staring up into his smiling face.

It did take several evenings, several dinners, several trips by Jozzy and her husband, Alan, down to the basement office where the two men paused their friendship and resumed the role-playing of 'job interview,' before Jocelyn was ready. Confident. "Eyes!" Suzanne would hear Alan demand over and over as she graded papers at the kitchen table. She couldn't help smiling to herself every time.

* * *

I thought maybe she was gonna forget. One day, she showed me. She take me to the middle school, where you know I work. She showed me the back. She showed me the front. She said this is the way if they hire you, that's where you're gonna work. And then she went. She talked to one of those guys who do the hiring. And after that, she come in. She took me to Jefferson, where Sutherland High School is. She took me to Lomb Building and I sat inside. I started to fill the application right there. She helped me fill the application, and then walk out. And I said to her, and I don't know, I can feel it. I feel something. I said to her, 'I will never forget this.' She said, 'it's not me. You did it.' I didn't know. I didn't know nothing because I didn't

know this area. I said, 'I don't know this area. I don't know anything.'
'This is all for you.' I said, 'It's gonna be a very, very long time from
now, I'm gonna mention your name.' And when they interviewed me,
they interviewed nine people. Nine people they interviewed, and I got
the job.

XLV. Pittsford

I'm the type of guy, I like to follow God's lead. Anything happen, it happen in His power. That's what he wants. And you cannot fight it. I been following His lead ever since I was very little, but I really and completely understand it when I was adult. Because I have seen some of miracle things God have done for me. And don't forget to mention His name, because He is a very generous guy. All He needs from us is a compliment. Whether you win or lose, I will say thank you to Him. Always say thanks to Him because, number one, He gives you life that you can never put a price on it. I mean, what else? You don't need nothing else. What else more you want? I don't know anything about Pittsford. You will get excitement, sometimes you don't see nothing in front of you and you wake up happy. You wake up feeling good. And there's something, some type of benediction and God gives it to you. Some of thoughts, some type of way he breathes over you. Once that happens, you have no choice but to be happy and feeling good at that moment. It's almost like you're happy and you don't know why you're happy. You know? I don't know Pittsford. I have never been on Monroe Avenue. And I don't know over there that way. You know, I've never been over that way. I don't even know there was a Monroe Avenue that way. Suzanne showed me everything. She showed me that way. And she teach me. And look at today, every little corner you tell me in Pittsford, if you give it to me, I'm gonna find it.

253

Tom held Jocelyn's file out in front of him as he showed his newest underling around the building. "It says here your name is '*Joyslin?*' but you go by 'Josh', is that right?"

"Yes!" Josh beamed. "My American name, "JOSH!" He said it with great emphasis and pride, embracing the name's simplicity.

"Well, good to have you, JOSH," Tom echoed teasingly.

"Oh, well is SO good to be here, thank you, THANK YOU, yes!" Josh trailed. His eyes were taking in every corner, every locker, every door up and down the broad halls.

"School starts next week. Since you'll be working nights, you'll just be coming in at the end of the kids' school day, lucky guy," Tom joked. Josh could tell they would get along beautifully.

"Oh, I love the kids, that okay whenever I work," Josh offered.

"We'll see how you do, buddy," Tom continued. "Down the road with a little seniority, you can switch to days if you'd like."

"Sound good, *buddy!*" Josh returned. He would never shake the practice of actively adopting up others' speech and putting it to use immediately.

His first week, Josh saw the occasional teacher come in and out of the building in the late afternoons and evenings he was there. Everyone always greeted him with a smile, and many people introduced themselves to him when they realized his was a new face. Universally, staff members were immediately taken with this vivacious creature. A few even noted, "Oh, yes, Suzanne *told* me about you! We're so happy to have you here!" The principal, Mr. Zona, made a point of introducing himself, saying, "You need anything, you come to me, okay Josh?" Josh was mesmerized.

At the start of the second week, on his arrival at 3:00 p.m., Josh finally got to see some of the students milling around. The school day was over, but it became immediately clear that there were many comings and goings in the hours after dismissal. It was magical. There was laughter in the halls every day. The kids were so playful and merry. Everyone carried such a big bag of books home, and Josh rejoiced for them in their opportunity to learn *so much, so young.* He could not stop himself from becoming a part of it if he had wanted to. "Hey buddy!". "How ARE you, princess?" he would remark as the kids passed him by. "I'm Mr. Josh," he would tell anyone who gave him their attention. "Nice to meet you!"

"Nice to meet you, too!" they would always return, some more shyly than others.

Just like at Blossom, Josh's reputation spread like wildfire among the teachers, even before he had been there long. Many had heard of the 'New Haitian custodian' and made eager to meet him once he was described. Josh learned his duties quickly and settled into his nightly routine.

One night a young health teacher named Mike passed Josh late in the afternoon as he was leaving his classroom.

"You must be Josh," Mike asked, giving Josh a friendly handshake.

"That's me, I'm Josh!" He remembered to say, "Nice to meet you!"

"I'm Mike, and I've got to tell you," Mike lowered his voice conspiratorially. "We teachers kind of fight over having *you* clean our classrooms."

Josh gave a great belly laugh. "Really?" He was quite taken aback.

"Absolutely! Keep up the great work." Then, the young man shot back over his shoulder as he walked away, stage whispering as he pointed at his classroom door, "And don't forget: 308."

* * *

Suzanne answered her phone brusquely at 10:30 on Thanksgiving morning. She was juggling a turkey in the oven, potatoes boiling on the stove, and pumpkin pie filling in the mixer.

"You will *never* guess what I'm doing, Suzanne!" she heard Jozzy practically sing through the line. She smiled.

"What are you doing, Jozzy?"

"I am sitting on my couch and I am watching TV and I am getting PAID. Nobody EVER pay me to sit at home and watch TV on my couch in all my life, Suzanne, and I owe this to *you*, God bless you! Can you tell how big I am smiling?"

"Yep, Jozzy. I can tell how big you are smiling. You enjoy your day off. You have *earned* it."

* * *

Dreams of the well came less frequently, though Josh believed God continued to reveal a plan to him through other images in his mind's eye. Over the years, Josh came to think of so many of these teachers as his friends. He moved to the day shift and had even more opportunity to interact with the kids. He found himself imparting wisdom to any who would listen, and especially emphasizing how profound the concepts of gratitude and respect were in his life. Teachers offering curriculum on subjects ranging from immigration, to perseverance, to well-being would invite "Mr. Josh" to come share his story with their classrooms, and this helped the students to recognize that a chat with Mr. Josh could be as therapeutic as a chat with their counselor, their parent, a friend.

Josh paid particular attention to any students who seemed down. Through many conversations, he began to understand the stark difference in how he had been raised and how some of these children were being raised, and he adopted a firm understanding of the root of happiness. He grew up in abject poverty, yet was trained to be grateful – not just *feign* gratitude, but actually feel it, for the mere breath in his lungs. Many of these children wanted for nothing, yet nobody had taught them that it was just as important to be *thankful* in their hearts for their bounty, and therefore they could not learn how to be happy. Sharing this discovery became his passion, although finding just the right words to do so was agonizing. He never pressed into the children's lives unless invited, but still went out of his way to at least brighten their day with a joke, a smile, a pat on the back.

For several years, while Josh still worked the evening shift, he would rise early and drive a taxi. His navigational skills never quite caught up with his ability to hustle, but he had an easy solution to this conundrum.

"I'm new here, so I can give you a discount if you tell me how to go," Josh would tell his fares, fully ten years after he had moved to Rochester. Nobody doubted this story given his heavy accent, and he was at peace with God in his little white lie, knowing the added income helped him support his Maman, now that he was in touch with her again.

When Josh was offered the day shift at Pittsford Middle School, his circle of work opportunities widened even more. He carried, and generously dispensed cards procured at "Staples" with his pager number, and later cell phone number, advertising the wealth of services he offered. Teachers had him come to mulch their flower beds year after year. Parents submitted to his charmingly persistent requests to clear their fall leaves. He always accepted dinner invitations from families, recognizing his duty to allow others to do for him as cheerfully as he always did for them, not to mention how personally gratified he was to share his life story, which he so often was asked to do. But his compulsion to work cost him dearly in his personal life at times. Women might feel initially attracted to Josh's desire to earn, but ultimately marginalized or all but forgotten in that very pursuit. Here again, he felt God was at peace with the ways he could give back, but encountered much less acceptance by mere mortal women. He could not help the disappointment he felt in them and in himself with the only sense of failure he experienced during this time in his life.

In 2004, his sister Anne Marie, was nearing the end of her life in Miami. Elianise had sponsored her immigration some years earlier, before her own return to Haiti and ultimate passing. "Josh, you're such a nice guy. I feel your pain. So go ahead and take as much time as you need to take care of what you need to take care," Principal Zona told him. Though they had not grown up together, Anne Marie

259

entrusted Jocelyn with her final arrangements; they had an emotional farewell before she was called to God, and Josh returned to his adopted family, emotionally overwrought. But a flood of cards with truly heartfelt sentiments of sorrow greeted him on his return, and he was restored. When a nagging back injury which he had only exacerbated with years of hard work demanded surgery in 2008, the flood was repeated. He was visited in the hospital and at home by many, many friends, including the young health teacher who had become principal and bore cards written by students and staff as well as many gifts from his Barker Road family. The first birthday celebration he had ever enjoyed in his entire life – his 40th – was orchestrated by a teacher named Sonia. Josh was beyond touched.

Anne Marie had been the last of his living siblings by his mother and father both. She was the only one he had the privilege of being with in their last days, adding to the poignancy of her death. But Josh was surrounded by a new family. A family which even his imaginative dreams of a *pays étranger* could not have foretold.

XLVI.   Home

When I was here in Rochester, let me see if I go to church here. I visit a lot of churches. I visit one church called, I think, St. Michael on Joseph Avenue. I think it's a Spanish church. Yes. Because that boy who in that church, I used to go to school at nighttime called Family Learning Center, and he invite me to that church for quite some time. And it's a beautiful church. And also, there's another church on Clinton Avenue and Clifford. I go to that church too and I visit. And after that, I don't go to any other church until I joined that church called St. Ambrose. St. Ambrose right there on Empire and Culver. I've been going there probably going on 12 or 13 years. Every one of 'em, they know me over there too. I do a lot of stuff over there too. I do little jobs for the church. I know one of those nuns, a long time ago, probably five or six years ago, but she retired from that position. And I know another lady who was a pastor. Her name was Laurie. And she just retired last year. But we have a lot of wonderful people out there. But I would have never sit down, explain to them my story, my background. But when we do get together to do our garden club for the church, to make it looking good and get together and do a little meeting what we're gonna do for that season, we do talk and have a wonderful time together.

I stopped making cards for myself, maybe two years ago. I'm going to tell you how I meet one of these rich women. I meet a rich woman – she come on Park Avenue while I was doing some work for someone, and she was walking. I said, 'Man, there's nothing like such a beautiful day, and watch a beautiful woman walking, a nice clean street, and you happen to see awesome guy like me, Josh, who can make your yard looking beautiful just like you.' I say, "Can I give you my card?" I'm still working for her right now. She have one of those huge house down by the lake. But two years ago I stopped making cards because I end up having, like, too much customer, because too many people – I think they tell each other.

Work in Pittsford was only a part of Josh's life. He and God had an understanding that if he wasn't able to attend church on any given Sunday because he had an opportunity to work, he would make it up with prayer and the collection basket. He became an entrepreneur. Through the Learning Center and his dancing he had met many other immigrants from the Caribbean, South America, and Mexico who were learning English and desperate to feed their families. So bountiful were Josh's Pittsford friends (and ensuing jobs) that he could invite his newly immigrated friends to come and help, and pay them a wage that reflected their hard work just as *he* had enjoyed as a migrant worker. He earned his United States citizenship. And he danced. He would never give up dancing. His club years were far behind him, but Josh now knew many others in his neighborhood that shared his passion for dancing and his love of their new lifestyle. They performed for fund raisers, school projects, and even appeared in the local paper. Whether near his downtown home or in the suburbs where he worked, more people than not had at least *heard* of this Haitian immigrant with boundless energy. Still, Josh imagined more.

"Hey, how about you find Josh a wife?" he joked one day with Principal Pero.

"Josh, something tells me you would have *no* trouble doing that on your own," was Mike's simple reply.

Josh produced his trademark laugh.

* * *

Josh did learn the joys of marriage. His wife would be the introvert to Josh's extroversion. She was the petite frame to Josh's powerful build. The shrewd skeptic to the trusting, eternal optimist. A professional unsure that she would meet a man who could be a partner. Although Josh may have sugar-coated his addiction to work before they were married, he had found just the woman who would embrace the simple life he could offer in nooks and crannies of time. Her fierce independence matched his. Her spirituality matched his. And for all his energy spent outside the home, both were people for whom family was everything. *IS* everything.

Moreover, Josh was the sort of *parent* to his children that his mother taught him to be. Ever the protective father, he bestowed upon them comfort, security, the gift of gratitude to God, and the power of work. In truth, work kept him from them more than he knew to be ideal, but just as he loved his mother for the work she did to feed her children, he labored every day with love in his heart for each of them, never doubting he was sharing the lesson that had meant the most in his own childhood.

XLVII. Earthquake

I just sat down to have a 5:00 break at the school. Well, I just turned the TV to the CNN. I was just turning the TV on as I sat down. And actually, it was on all the channels. And then they was coming with the breaking news, and all this stuff happened over there in Haiti. Right away, I tried to call. And I forgot about taking a break for a second. I went to call and I couldn't get in. And then, later on, I got in. They have little damage from what's left over at their house. And also, it was a big crack right in the middle of their floor, the dirt floor in their house. And then, later on, I found out and fix it. But I did talk to them later in that day and that night after I came home. The reaction in the school, everybody was almost like, the way I could describe to you, it's almost like when we had September 11th. Everybody was talking. Because anybody have something to say what we're gonna do. And the principal and everybody said what are we gonna do to help Haiti. They're gonna come up with something to help Haiti. We already have a church right there near Four Corners Pittsford. They've been helping Haiti for years. I went there. I did a dance for them over there for the money they wanna raise for Haiti one time. And I think they raised like, I think $9,000 or $10,000. Yes. They raised to help Haiti with all the stuff they did. But after that, the school reaction was big. It was amazing. Everybody, the kids, when they saw me, everybody say, 'how was your family?' Did you talk to

'em? Are they doing OK?' They're all very caring. Very caring and
they give you the support when they know you need it the most.

Pittsford Middle School had been the largest school in the
district. Backward from most districts, where the *high* school
represented the largest convergence of feeder schools, Pittsford
Middle School had been comprised of *all* the students in the Pittsford
Central School District during their 6th, 7th and 8th grade years, then
the population split to attend one of two separate high schools. For
Josh's first ten years, therefore, he truly had the opportunity to get to
know EVERY child in Pittsford in that age bracket.

In the fall of 2006, a brand-new, *second* middle school opened
its doors. Health teacher, Mike Pero, took the helm of the older
building which was then dubbed "Barker Road Middle School." The
friendly rivalry that existed between the two high schools now
trickled down to the middle schools. Mr. Pero, who had a true
passion for the social-emotional development of his charges, was
excited at his opportunity to reach more students as principal. And he
consoled himself that even if he did not have the shiniest facility, he
certainly had many great assets among his staff, not the least of which
was Josh. The new "Barker Road Family" took shape over the
ensuing years; a warm yet focused ambiance infused the halls.

In year four of Mr. Pero's tenure, on January 12, 2010, a 7.0-
magnitude earthquake gripped Port-au-Prince, Haiti. On January 13,

2010, he had the privilege of discovering just how amazing his students were.

The halls were abuzz with worry. Students who caught sight of him in the halls would stop him to ask, "Mr. Pero, do you know if Josh's family is alright? We should do something to help them – to help other people in Haiti, too!" Mike was moved by their concern for the beloved custodian, their global thinking, their empathy. And he was not one to miss out on an educational opportunity.

After learning that Josh's family, well outside the capital where the epicenter of the earthquake had been, were all safe, Mr. Pero posed a serious request to the inspirational man, who was clearly moving about his day a bit more slowly, a bit less jovially than usual.

"Josh, these kids love you, man." Josh smiled and nodded. "They are already taking up a penny drive, but I've got to tell you, those are not *pennies* I'm seeing in that jar! They want to help your family recover."

"That SO nice," Josh shook his head, deeply touched. "That so nice. I love these kids too, my friend. But my family good. Maybe that money can go to other Haitians who need help recover?" Josh submitted.

"Absolutely. That's a great idea," Mike countered. "And Josh... I was wondering if you would speak at an assembly of the whole school. You have done a great job talking with the kids in the classroom so I know you are comfortable in front of an audience," Mike donned a wry smile. Josh's comfort at the center of attention was well known. He managed a laugh, though it didn't come from his core as it so often did.

"Yeah, I do that. I happy to do that, no problem. What you want me to say?"

"You know, just talk about Haiti, what it was like for you growing up there. And, Josh, these kids could really benefit from understanding how it is that you manage to be such a positive guy. A happy person. We have great kids – this week has shown me how much they care. But, you know, I believe that hearing *you* explain what has helped you be strong, be committed, and always positive will go a long way with the students. Our faculty is teaching the students about the character trait of perseverance. You have modeled this trait and we would be honored to have you help our students understand the importance of this quality. Coming from YOU, I know that message will pack a lot of meaning," Mike finished.

"Yeah, sure, okay Mr. President. You should go be president of Haiti, Mr. Pero. You are such a great guy. A great boss. I will ask my wife. She can help me. She will help me organize some speech," Josh pondered.

"That's a great idea," Mike replied. Having met Josh's wife at their wedding, Mike was confident that Josh would come in with just what the kids needed to hear.

* * *

I have a story to tell. I know it is not like a lot of other people's story, and that's why I want it to be told. I am a real guy. I have done much I can be proud of, and also many things maybe I would do differently. I thank God for all the people I have known in my life. Every single one. I learn something from everyone I know. Some are part of this story for the world, and some are not.

Everything's flowers. Nothing's dying. And so, it's just like a rose garden where it gets water 24/7. Everything grow. There's nothing dying. Because, you know, you just plant the seed and then, all you're doing right now is you're watering. That's it. You're watering. But if you don't appreciate and you don't say thanks, you don't put no value in it. You just spread something with a lot of sun, hot temperatures. A lot of sun. You plant it just like you plant it in the sand, and the temperature is 100 degrees hot. You'll kill it. That's the only way I can describe it is you'll kill it.

* * *

Mr. Pero stood at a makeshift podium in the gymnasium – the only room in his building that could accommodate the entire student body. The acoustics were not ideal, but the school had come together as one to help a faraway country, and he wanted them to *stay* together as one to hear the wise words of their one tangible connection to that place in such great need. Josh. He raised his hand, which brought a substantial hush in comparison to the loud hum that had filled the room. It was enough to begin.

"Boys and girls…" he waited, and 900 students, 100 staff members came to a hush. They all knew why they were there.

"Boys and girls, you have really made me proud this week. Proud that you are demonstrating a global awareness by watching the news and taking an interest in things happening around you. Proud that you feel compelled to *act* when you see others in need. Oh, and, by the way, you have raised over *three thousand dollars* through the 'penny' drive…"

A cheer went up. Mr. Pero gave them their moment to celebrate. Finally he raised a hand again and the hush returned.

"Now, our friend, Mr. Josh," he gestured to Josh who stood behind him, nervously fidgeting with a stack of papers, "is so very grateful for what you have offered, but *his* family is doing pretty well, and he wants that money to go to help Haitians closer to the damage." Josh stepped forward, nodding vigorously.

"But boys and girls, I've asked Mr. Josh to talk with you today about his life in Haiti. I know the news has brought this interesting part of the world to the front of all our minds. Now, some of you, a lot of you,

270

I hope, have gotten to know Mr. Josh, and you know a little about his *personal* story. I'll ask you to give him your full attention and respect. And as you hear Josh speak, I ask that you think about the connections he is making with our newest core principle, 'perseverance'. From everything *I* have learned about this amazing man standing beside me, I know in my heart that this is a day that you will never forget."

With that, Mike gave Josh a hug, saying into his ear over the respectful clapping that filled the room, "Josh, you're going to do great. Just be yourself. You can't go wrong."

Josh took Mr. Pero's place at the microphone and beamed at the students. He held his papers where he could see them easily. His wife had made the font nice and big so he wouldn't need his glasses. Taking a cue from Mr. Pero, he raised his hand and the students immediately quieted. A rush of excitement, of oneness with these precious kids, filled his soul.

"My name is Jocelyn Apo. I was born in Haiti in a city called Cap Haitian. Haiti received its independence in 1804. It is still a poor country, but because of the recent disaster, it is getting the help it needs now.

"I am going to tell you about my family. My mom had five kids. I was raised by my mother and step-father, so all together I have eight brothers and sisters. However, I found my real father when I was 15 years old who was also a good support.

"Life in Haiti for my mother and father was great for a moment. But as I grew older I began to realize the struggles they really had. They had a hard time feeding us. With five kids and no job, it was very difficult for my mom and dad. I've seen my mother carry heavy things over her head and walk so far away from home to sell it just to make some money for the family to live on. Sometimes we would eat one time a day or went to bed without eating.

"My mom appreciated everything she had. She was also my best teacher and taught us to use what we had at home for learning about life. She told us to thank God for the food we had to eat and even when we didn't have food to eat to make sure we thank God for seeing another day.

"Now out of the five kids my mother had, four of them have passed away. My mother still thinks she was the cause of my one brother's death. One day she was going somewhere and he begged to go with her. My mother told him 'no you cannot go, stay here, I will be back.' My brother started crying. By the time my mother came back she found him lying on the floor not responding. She found out that he ate something bad. Until this day she does not really know what killed him, but she always felt bad for not taking him with her when she left home. They called the doctor to come over. The doctor told her that the baby ate something and that is what took the baby's life. To this day, my mother is still talking about this.

"Now as a young teenager and seeing my parents struggle to feed us, I started thinking about what I could do to help my family. By 15 years old, I already had in my mind that I was going to come to America. My older cousin was the leader of the idea. I did not leave Haiti until I was 19 years old. We talked about coming to America even to make a better life for ourselves, and then we decided to put our words into action.

"One day a group of us got together and went into the middle of the woods, where no one could hear us, and began cutting down trees. We had to cut down the trees, cut and shape the wood to make a plank, and we went on from there to build a boat. I don't really know how long it took, but it took a long time to build the boat.

"When I came to the US, I came on the boat with one sister and once cousin and a lot of friends. On October 5, 1980 at midnight, we left Haiti to come to America. We did not want anyone to see us. That was the first time I ever stayed out late"

Laughter erupted, fueling Josh's confidence.

"Sixty-two of us got into a 12 by 12 foot boat. The boat was not built with a motor. It had a sail and a paddle. We had a little food on board and a little water. A week later, everything that we brought with us on the boat was gone.

"Our first stop was Cuba, which is very close to Haiti. We stayed there for a few days. In order to eat, we exchanged our clothes, watches and other belongings for Carnation milk. We left Cuba and went on our way to the United States.

"During the day, the boat does not move much because we needed the wind to help us move faster. But every night we had a lot of wind which helped us to move very fast. Sometimes there is a lot of rain so we got very wet.

"We spent 18 days on the water. One day we saw a big ship which happened to be the US Coast Guard. They took all 62 of us into their ship. They gave each of soup to eat and soap – we took a shower for the first time in 18 days. Well, actually, they gave us a water hose to use for taking a shower.

"They picked us up at ten o'clock in the morning. They took us to Miami Beach. We got to Miami Beach at two o'clock in the morning. Then we got on the bus which took us to Key West.

"I came to America in 1980 and I thank God that I am here in the United States. I never saw any of the people from the boat again except my sister. Living in America can be difficult not knowing the language. I have asked God to help me learn the English language that I did not know as fast as possible. It was not easy. For example I went to the store to buy a loaf of bread. The cashier told me that she needed more money and I did not quite understand. So I left the bread in the store and went back home empty handed.

"I went to a Haitian school in Florida. It was very good because it would help me understand English better. I was able to ask questions and get the answers that I needed. My first job was in Florida. I worked for two weeks for a guy from Cuba who was building a swimming pool for someone. He wanted someone to take away the excess dirt. When I was done and went to get paid, the guy was gone and I never got paid.

"I also picked oranges, lemons, tomatoes and watermelon and cut sugar cane and celery in Florida. I did this for five years. While I was living in Florida, I traveled to New York State to Williamson, Sodus and Wolcott where I worked picking apples. I also traveled to Michigan to work picking raspberries, blueberries, apples and grapes. We also went to North Carolina and South Carolina picking tobacco, cucumbers and squash. Then after all of that we went back to Florida.

"Then, throughout the years, my English started getting better so I decided to stop doing migrant work. I then came to New York State to live for good.

"I came to Rochester in 1984. My first job was at Blossom Nursing Home. I worked there for five years. Then I worked in construction for three years. I have also worked as a taxi driver and did a lot of other jobs in between.

"One day I met a lady named Suzanne Robinson at the nursing home. She said that she was going to find me another job. And in 1996 I came to work for Pittsford School District.

"Students, I want to tell you that it is very important to work hard. I stand here today to tell you about my life so that you can understand that life can be fun, but it is important to listen and make the right decisions.

"Some things my mother taught me are to respect authority – respect all people no matter their age or what they look like. Respect your parents, teachers, principal. Remember never quit. Don't fight! Pay attention to the rules. No matter what you are going through or how difficult a time might seem, always remember: never, never quit. And remember you have love in your heart and *use it* at all times, especially when you need it most in times of trouble."

With that, this happy man, this beautiful man whom most only knew to be an effervescent presence with an exotic accent, cheerfully pushing a broom through the halls of their privileged school, openly wept. In response, the room, packed with nearly nine hundred adolescents between the ages of 11 and 14, and 100 plus teachers was nearly silent, with the exception of a tide of sniffles. From sixth grade girls still favoring pink for their daily wardrobe up to the eighth grade athletes, full of bravado on any other day, not a soul in the room appeared unmoved, nor even demonstrated embarrassment for their empathetic tears.

Josh collected himself. "My mother taught me – never go outside with your shirt or pants wrinkled…"

A new wave of laughter to relieve the palpable tension gripped the room. From this, Josh regained his joy, the winning smile he was most known for, and went on.

"She said 'never depend on nobody else to do anything for you'. Students, *please* take advantage of your education while you can. It was very difficult for my mom and dad with five kids to pay for our education. She sent us to school, but we had to drop out of school at a young age because she could not make the payments. She did not have enough money to feed us and at the same time to buy the uniforms, books, pencils or shoes. At that time it cost three dollars for each child to go to school, but money did not come easy.

"My step-father was very good to me. He taught me a lot at home. He taught me how to count, add, subtract and multiply by using stones.

"Now even through all my mother's struggles and difficult times, my mother still always told us *never to give up or quit* and to *always* pray to God. She always told us to pray to God anyway and thank Him for giving us a chance to see this beautiful day."

Josh glanced at the last of his notes and steeled himself. The love and encouragement of everyone in the room enveloped him like a warm blanket as he stood uncomfortably still with so many eyes on him. Josh was overwhelmed in the prior days by being the face of Haiti for these caring children, all with so much promise. It was almost more than he

277

could bear. Finding this family of teachers, students, and their parents was more than he might ever have imagined or prayed for throughout his many years of hard work, but he knew God had rewarded him for persevering.

At last, with only a futile effort to choke back his tears, he concluded, "I will never forget what my mother, step-father and father has done for me. I will always love them. Thank you, kids. Thank you for listening today."

Clapping built slowly in obvious deference for this emotional account, but quickly there was a roar of applause, punctuated only by the clack of wooden bleachers as their occupants – first teachers then students – scurried to their feet. Josh basked in this outpouring of support, and bowed his head. These were children familiar with the protocol of live performances, but should there be any question in the meaning of his gesture, all watched on as Josh acted on his mother's words which could not be drowned out. '*Croiser les bras*,' he felt her say as he made the sign of the cross in gratitude to God. Glancing back up, he clasped his hands together, shaking them vigorously in gratitude to his found family.

Afterword

There he was in the "Red Team" hall where I can always count on finding him when I pick up my daughter at dismissal. It was there where, almost two years ago, I told him I would be joining the project of telling his story. "I always know you were very busy here at school, I never have an idea you write a book too!" Josh was elated.

"Jocelyn!" I get his attention, and attempt in my rusty French, "Bon jour! Comment allez-vous?" He responds eloquently and I laugh and give up. He returns my laugh.

"We're almost done, Josh!" I tell him, handing him 20 more pages.

"We ARE?!" His big brown eyes pop out of his head and he gives me his trademark stage stance, bracing every part of his body.

"Yep!" I return gleefully.

"You know, I tell my Maman about the book. She SO happy. She pray for you too," he tells me, giving me a sly sideways glance, communicating that I am special.

"That's really sweet. How is she doing?"

"Oh, not so good. She got a bad tooth. My niece take her to see a dentist though. You know, I call her and my niece know – she got to answer *right away* and I keep sending money," he laughs, though this laugh carries authority with it that I can see he doesn't mind exerting in the pursuit of taking care of Maman.

"I call her!" he chimes, whipping his phone out of his pocket. "You talk to her!"

Embarrassed, I agree. One doesn't tell Josh no, as evidenced by my role in this project.

He places the phone on 'speaker' and holds it in front of him. A woman answers. He rattles off a few phrases in Creole, and she responds. An exchange. Then a pregnant pause. "She's getting her. She not so good. She in pain," he says to me in a whispered voice.

"Allo? Amos?" a low, gravelly but frail voice comes through the line.

"Allo Maman!" Josh proceeds to tell her that I am here. That I am helping with the book. I watch him, I am nervous to speak to Amancia. She is only a legend in my mind. Not really flesh and blood. Finally he cues me, 'Say hello!' he urges.

"Allo, Amancia! Je suis Julie. J'écris le livre avec Jocelyn." I'm out. She replies slowly, I can tell every syllable is an effort, but I don't understand and search Josh's face for help.

"She says thank you," he whispers. "She says she will pray for you."

"Merci," I attempt.

Josh resumes. I watch his faraway gaze through glassy eyes as he rubs his freshly shaven head. They have several exchanges in Creole. I have never seen this expression before or since, in all the conversations we have had to prepare his life story.

Cover art by Rose Szmutko

Photo by Janice Mix